KEZIAH WARNER is a playwright and dramaturg based in Melbourne. She won Sydney Theatre Company's Patrick White Playwrights Award, has been shortlisted for the Griffin Award, the Martin Lysicrates Prize, the Rodney Seaborn Playwrights Award and the Max Afford Award, and longlisted for Soho Theatre's Young Writers' Award. Her credits include: *Poona* (Next Wave, 2021), *Control* (Red Stitch Actors' Theatre, 2019), *Help Yourself* (MTC's Cybec Electric, 2019), *Luna* (VCA, 2019), and *Her Father's Daughter* (Hotel Now, 2018). Keziah is an alumna of Melbourne Theatre Company's Women in Theatre Program, Malthouse Theatre's Besen Family Artist Program, Red Stitch Actors' Theatre's INK Program, Playwriting Australia's Post-Production Program, and Soho Theatre's Writer's Lab, UK. *Hour of the Wolf*, a new immersive show created with Matthew Lutton, will premiere at Malthouse Theatre in 2023.

NOSFERATU

Keziah Warner

CURRENCY PRESS
The performing arts publisher

CURRENCY PLAYS

First published in 2023
by Currency Press Pty Ltd,
PO Box 2287, Strawberry Hills, NSW, 2012, Australia
enquiries@currency.com.au
www.currency.com.au

Typeset by Brighton Gray for Currency Press.
Cover photograph by Kristian Gehradte. Cover shows Jacob Collins-Levy. Cover
design by Mathias Johansson for Currency Press.

Currency Press acknowledges the Traditional Owners of the Country on which
we live and work. We pay our respects to all Aboriginal and Torres Strait
Islander Elders, past and present.

A catalogue record for this
book is available from the
National Library of Australia

Contents

'you are now to me flesh of my flesh, blood of my blood, kin of my kin, my bountiful wine-press for a while'
Dracula, Bram Stoker

Nosferatu was first performed on 10 February 2023 at Malthouse Theatre, Melbourne, with the following cast:

TOM	Keegan Joyce
ELLEN	Shamita Siva
KATE BULWER	Sophie Ross
JAMES KNOCK	Max Brown
COUNT ORLOK	Jacob Collins-Levy

Director, Bridget Balodis
Dramaturg, Mark Pritchard
Production Dramaturg, Bernadette Fam
Set and Costume Designer, Romanie Harper
Lighting Designer, Paul Jackson
Composer & Sound Designer, Kelly Ryall
Intimacy Choreographer, Cessalee Stovall
Stage Manager, Cecily Rabey
Assistant Stage Manager, Harry Dowling

CHARACTERS

TOM, a mayoral staffer, late 20s.

ELLEN, a journalist, late 20s.

KATE BULWER, a doctor, early 40s.

JAMES KNOCK, former miner now reluctant mayor, early 40s.

COUNT ORLOK, the money, 600 give or take.

SHIP'S CAPTAIN, voice only

RESPONDER, voice only

SETTING

Bluewater, a small former-mining town, Western Tasmania.

NOTES

Words in (brackets) are unspoken.

We can see characters who aren't in a scene existing in their own space while another scene plays out. A sense of the town, the community, coexisting.

Beats are shorter, but more charged, than pauses.

PROLOGUE

Bluewater. A desolate place.

Night. KATE, *alone. She's clutching a book.*

KATE: You don't know the truth.

You've heard the rumours, the whispers of what happened here. The name conjures images in your mind now. One of those cursed places.

But I was there.

My hometown: Bluewater, Tasmania.

We were unremarkable once.

Population ageing, hills barren, water running ruin. Just a mining town with no mine.

Then one day, a stranger came to town. You've heard the story. You know it's only tragedy that puts you on the map.

I'll try to tell you what happened. What I saw. The question is if you can believe. Believe in things you know to be untrue.

Nosferatu.

That word. That sound. That bewitching agony. It's a winged thing, a deathbird, a siren. If you listen, you can hear it, calling your name in the night.

To resist is almost unbearable.

But please, if you let it in, the pictures of your life will fade to shadows, nightmares will crawl from your heart and evil will feed on your blood.

If you let it in, you will see things, you will do things you never thought possible.

Perhaps now, we see she is also holding a bloodied knife.

If you believe nothing else, believe that.

Beware the call: nosferatu.

Please. Save yourselves.

It's too late for me.

ACT ONE

Day. KNOCK, TOM *and* ELLEN *in* KNOCK*'s office.* KNOCK *is engrossed in a printed report.*

TOM: We need more time.

ELLEN: I brought it to you as soon as I could.

KNOCK: It's the / wording.

TOM: We'd like to speak to the scientists.

ELLEN: I'm not even supposed to have it, they can't know I brought it to you.

KNOCK: 'Plant life in Bluewater is practically non-existent.'

TOM: How long till this goes public?

ELLEN: They'll submit to the board end of the month.

TOM: So we have a few weeks.

KNOCK: And this. This venus flytrap thing:

ELLEN: I'm going to print tomorrow.

TOM: Saying what?

ELLEN: That this is the final nail in the coffin.

TOM: You can't do that.

KNOCK: 'The dearth of nutrients in the soil has forced an unprecedented evolution to carnivorism.'

TOM: You can't announce the mine won't reopen before we have a plan.

ELLEN: So would you like to comment?

TOM: We're not making a statement yet.

ELLEN: People will want to hear from the mayor's office.

KNOCK: 'Carnivorism'!

TOM: We're still trying to secure new investment.

ELLEN: This is about the mass poisoning of land. The town deserves to know.

KNOCK: It's meant to be an environmental impact study. Not *Night of the Living Dead.*

TOM: I'm not saying don't publish anything. Just, not everything. Not yet.

ELLEN: So keep lying?

KNOCK: Since when has evolution been a bad thing?

ELLEN: What?

KNOCK: The flytrap. 'Unprecedented evolution.'

TOM: Right, exactly. That's a story. You could publish that.

ELLEN: 'Toxic earth births mutant'?

TOM: If this plant can survive then so can others. It's a sign of hope.

KNOCK: 'Bluewater turns green'.

ELLEN: That's not what the report is saying.

TOM: Come on. A carnivore? A meat-eating plant? That's got you written all over it.

ELLEN: 'Bluewater produces ravenous monster.'

TOM: Spin it however you like. Just give us a few more weeks to find new investment.

ELLEN: Tom, it's been two years.

TOM: Two years since the last collapse. We've only had control of the land for a month.

ELLEN: Convenient the board finally handed that over right before this report came out.

TOM: They want us to have options.

ELLEN: They're based in Berlin and Guangzhou. You think they care about some tiny mine in Nowhere, Tasmania?

KNOCK: This is why we need local investment. Someone who can see there are lives here worth investing in. That people can mean more than profit.

ELLEN: So someone who doesn't understand about capitalism?

TOM: There's interest. We had a letter this morning.

KNOCK: We did?

> TOM *starts trying to find the letter. Trying to remember what it said.*

TOM: Yes, someone from … / Sydney, or …

ELLEN: So promising you forgot about it.

TOM: No it's … He said … Here.

> TOM *hands the letter to* ELLEN.

ELLEN: Christ, it's written in some sort of satanic code.

TOM: That's called handwriting.

ELLEN: How can you even read this?

TOM: It's a lead.

KNOCK: Let me see.

> ELLEN *hands the letter to* KNOCK.

ELLEN: Look, I'd prefer to get a quote, but I can go to print without you.

TOM: People's lives are more important than your front page, Ellen.

> KNOCK *is entranced by the letter.*

ELLEN: Their lives are gone / already.

TOM: Exactly. We've already lost everything. Not just our jobs. Our homes, our futures. You've seen what we've gone through the last two years. Knock. My dad. My brother.

ELLEN: / That's not fair.

TOM: And now we are literally haemorraging people. If we don't do something soon

ELLEN: The town will die, I know.

TOM: All we have left is hope. Do you want to be the one to take that away?

> KNOCK *faints.*

SCENE TWO

Later that day. KNOCK *in Kate's GP clinic.*

KATE: I'll need to take some blood.

KNOCK: I was afraid you'd say that.

KATE: Painless, I promise.

KNOCK: I wasn't going to bother you. Tom / sort of insisted.

KATE: No it's good you / came in …

KNOCK: And I haven't seen you yet, since you've / been back so …

KATE: I've been meaning to say hi, I've just / been busy with

KNOCK: You remember Tom? He would have only been / about ten or …

KATE: He's my neighbour / now.

KNOCK: You're at your mum's house, of course. How is she?

KATE: They moved her to palliative care. So. I go to see her, every day.

KNOCK: It's good you're here.
KATE: Sleeping in my teenage bedroom.
KNOCK: Right.
KATE: Memories.
KNOCK: Yeah.

> *Beat.* KATE *holds up the needle.* KNOCK *offers his arm and looks away. She takes his blood.*

You must find it slow here, compared (with Melbourne)
KATE: Peaceful.
KNOCK: We're pleased to have you. Since Dr Morgan left people have been having to drive over an hour.
KATE: They're a bit suspicious of my surname.
KNOCK: Not at all.
KATE: 'You're not Lillian's Bulwer's daughter are you?'
KNOCK: That's them being friendly.
KATE: She's still town pariah.
KNOCK: It's not all miners versus greenies anymore. If we could turn the mine into one big solar panel, we would.
KATE: You just trying to make me feel better?
KNOCK: I would never.

> *Beat.* KATE *marks up the blood sample.*

How does it look?
KATE: It's red, which is a good start.
KNOCK: You really are a doctor.
KATE: If you're really a mayor.
KNOCK: Someone had to step up.
KATE: I wanted to talk to you actually.
KNOCK: You did?
KATE: About money.
KNOCK: / Oh.
KATE: The last guy scrapped bulk billing and people can barely afford appointments. So if there's any / sort of funding or
KNOCK: Now isn't really a great time / to be looking for
KATE: No of course I / just thought
KNOCK: Everyone really needs money / at the moment so
KATE: I just thought there's no harm / in asking.

KNOCK: I should go. There's lots of work I / have to …

KATE: You should try to get some rest. It's no wonder you're / fainting if you're

KNOCK: It's good to see you, Kate. Dr Bulwer.

KATE: Come back. If it gets worse.

SCENE THREE

That night. Ellen and Tom's house. ELLEN *is smoking out of the back door and reading—the book from the Prologue. She's ashing into something concealable, like a tin with a lid. She hears something.*

ELLEN: Shit.

> *She stubs out the cigarette, puts the butt in the tin and hides the tin. She eats a mint (or similar) and sprays air freshener. There's a hurried but routine feel to it. She sits at the table with the book.*
>
> TOM *enters. He's holding a bunch of roses at his side.*

Listen to this: 'From the seed of Belial himself sprang an unholy creature that liveth in sinister caves, tombes'—with an 'e' on the end—'and coffins, which are filled with cursed haunting dirt from the fields of The Black Death. / At night'—

TOM: Ellen.

ELLEN: 'this vile [*maybe she sounds nosferatu out?*] nosferatu digs his claws into his victims and suckles himself on the hellish elixir of their bloode'—also / with an 'e'.

TOM: Can we …

ELLEN: 'Beware that his shadow does not engulf you like a daemonic nightmare.' Guess how many 'e's in daemonic. It's both more and less / than you'd think.

TOM: What the fuck are you reading?

ELLEN: *Of Daemons, Unearthly Phantomes and Things Unknowable.* Kate was throwing it out. Are those roses?

TOM: No.

ELLEN: You know how I feel about florists.

TOM: You don't trust them.

ELLEN: They kill the thing they love.

TOM: We all feel like that sometimes.

ELLEN: It wasn't personal.

TOM: A heads-up might have been nice.

ELLEN: We agreed. Separation of church and state.

TOM: Not when you're about to drop a bombshell.

ELLEN: I was being professional.

TOM: By humiliating me?

ELLEN: I didn't have to bring it to you at all.

TOM: It's so terrifying to me that you think that.

ELLEN: I'm trying to prepare people for the inevitable.

TOM: Don't pretend this is some sort of altruistic / public service.

ELLEN: I care about the truth.

TOM: You care about your work getting national attention.

ELLEN: And you just want to be a hero, so.

TOM: I'm trying to make things right. For the town, for my parents.

ELLEN: And I need to let people know I still exist. We're not going to live here forever. You want me to die writing the fucking word jumble?

TOM: No-one's / dying.

ELLEN: Every single one of you is in denial.

Maybe you need something, someone, to shock you into action.

Beat. TOM *hands the flowers to* ELLEN *and starts to walk out of the room.*

TOM: Happy anniversary.

ELLEN: Tom.

He stops. Any normal person would apologise here.

Did you know we import most of our roses from Kenya? If you wanted to support local industry you could have just picked one of the flytraps.

TOM: You know what?

He takes the flowers back.

ELLEN: Don't! I was joking.

She grabs for them. As she pulls them, a thorn catches TOM'*s thumb.*

TOM: Ow fuck.

ELLEN: You okay?

TOM: I'm fine.

ELLEN: You're bleeding.

TOM: It's fine.

ELLEN: Come here.

TOM: No.

ELLEN: Give me your fucking hand!

> *Beat. He does, reluctantly. She kisses his hand then sucks the blood from his thumb.*

I'll wait. To publish the report.

> TOM *stops himself saying 'thank you'.*

TOM: … I'm going to Sydney.

ELLEN: Great. Finally. When do we leave?

TOM: Yeah / very funny.

ELLEN: Sydney is smart actually. You hate Melbourne, I hate here. Neutral territory.

TOM: El. I'm going to meet this investor?

ELLEN: The kook with the handwriting? What's his deal?

TOM: Unfortunately I have to keep his identity a secret and only tell you when it's far too late and there's nothing you can do about it.

ELLEN: Don't be like that.

TOM: He's just … interested in the land. That's all.

ELLEN: So like property development … ? Oil? Media empire? Tech? Pharma? Arms dealing? Blood diamonds?

TOM: You'll laugh.

ELLEN: I won't. I promise.

TOM: He's … old money.

ELLEN: What's funny about that?

TOM: Calls himself a count.

ELLEN: … What the fuck? Like the title? Count?

TOM: That's / laughing.

ELLEN: Like aristocracy? Like the Count of / Monte Cristo?

TOM: Yeah okay. Fuck this.

ELLEN: Like the count off *Sesame / Street*?

TOM: I'm going to bed.

ELLEN: It's six o'clock.

TOM: I know it sounds ridiculous. I know, okay? But we are running out of time and this guy actually wants to meet us, to engage, and maybe it's a joke / to you but

ELLEN: I don't think / it's a joke.

TOM: This matters to me.

ELLEN: And I think he'll love you. And everything will work out.

TOM: [*turning away*] No you don't.

ELLEN: [*drawing him back*] Knock's not going?

TOM: We decided it's better if it's just me. I decided. You know what Knock's like.

ELLEN: Desperate? Just wants to be told what to do?

TOM: I think he'd sell his soul at this point.

ELLEN: And you're going to play hardball are you?

TOM: I can be tough.

ELLEN: You're so cute.

TOM: Fuck off.

ELLEN: This guy is just gonna eat you up.

TOM: Let's hope so.

ELLEN: I like the flowers

TOM: No, you don't.

ELLEN: Tom. Really.

> *She starts biting the heads off the flowers, spitting them out.*

They're delicious.

> *She moves towards him, wrecking the flowers. As she gets close, he grabs her. They kiss.*

SCENE FOUR

KATE *in a room in a palliative care home. Her mum—Lillian Bulwer— is on a ventilator, unconscious. During the following,* KNOCK *enters, unseen by* KATE. *He's holding a plant, like an iris, in a pot.*

KATE: I've been walking up to the tarn, before work. The water's even bluer than I remember. Practically glowing. You know, I read something. About copper. Did you know this? It's essential in building electric cars. I wanted to tell you. Maybe the mine could have been something good.

> Everything feels like it's happening too late. Like you're missing it. That's normal.

> You remember I did that secondment in palliative care? So. Practically an expert.

This is the longest conversation we've had in a while.
I'm sorry I wasn't (around more) —

KNOCK *makes himself known—maybe he coughs or says her name.*

Shit.

KNOCK: Sorry.

KATE: James, how long have you been … ?

KNOCK: Not long.

KATE: I was / just

KNOCK: Yes, it's meant to be good isn't it? Talking.

Beat.

KATE: You're holding a plant.

KNOCK: Right. I uh I brought it.

He kind of thrusts the plant at KATE.

It's a flytrap.

KATE: Okay.

KNOCK: We've just discovered / that this

KATE: Oh, yes, I just read Ellen's article about this.

KNOCK: I thought you'd (like it).

KATE: I do.

KNOCK: I mean, I thought Lillian would.

KATE: No, yeah. Plants on the attack? She'd love it. Thank you.

KNOCK: You're welcome.

KATE: Should you be … ? Aren't they studying this? You probably shouldn't be digging these up.

KNOCK: Oh. No. Perk of the job.

Beat.

Do you want to get dinner?

KATE: Oh, um …

KNOCK: Or …

KATE: I'm quite busy. With work. And / mum, so …

KNOCK: No, I mean. I meant, you should eat. You should, I could bring you something. You should look after yourself.

KATE: Thought I was the doctor.

KNOCK: It's just, what you were saying, before …

KATE: I was talking to her.

KNOCK: I didn't mean to (pry) … I just. If you want someone to talk to, who's …

KATE: Conscious.

KNOCK: Yeah.

KATE: … Okay.

KNOCK: Okay?

KATE: Let's get dinner.

KNOCK: That's …

KATE: I could use a friend.

KNOCK: … Great.

SCENE FIVE

Night. ELLEN *asleep on the sofa. She's having a nightmare. Her phone rings. It goes to voicemail.*

VOICEMAIL: Message received: nine-twenty-five p.m.

TOM: Hey it's me, I finally landed in Sydney. I'm on like two percent so I might cut out. We sat on the tarmac for five hours because of weather. And I don't have a number to let this guy know I'm late so, fuck, hopefully he's still awake when I—

Message cuts out.

VOICEMAIL: Message received: eleven-forty-two p.m.

TOM: Hey babe, I'm charging my phone in a pub. So apparently this mansion is in some sort of taxi blackout or something. I got a train, then a bus and I'm still half an hour away so I asked in this pub if there was anywhere I could get a cab and swear to god they looked at me like I was out of my mind when I said where I was going. Some bloke at the bar has said he could give me a lift to the bottom of the hill but not to the house itself. I thought I was going to the big city but apparently I've gone back in time. Okay I love you. I'll let you know when I get there. Unless I'm dead. Okay bye.

End of message.

VOICEMAIL: Message received: twelve-thirty-one a.m.

TOM: I'm walking up a fucking hill now. The driver guy crossed himself. Like actually—

He crosses himself.

What the fuck? And fleeced me for like a month's rent. I could see the house before but there are trees now, I don't remember seeing them when I was, like a forest. And there's a lot of cloud or mist or something and what the ... I've definitely ... okay there's a signpost, like a ye olde ... I swear I've passed that already. I'm walking in fucking circles here.

Howling.

What on ... babe, do they have dingoes in Sydney?

Howling gets louder.

Okay this place is creepy / as—
ORLOK: Hello Tom.
TOM: Fuck! Oh Jesus Christ I—

Message cuts out.

SCENE SIX

The same. TOM *on the phone.* ORLOK *behind him. He's grey-haired, hunched over, desiccated.*

(Note: if previous scene is audio, repeat opening here live. If previous scene is live, merge into this scene and jump straight to 'I've startled you.')

TOM: Okay this place is creepy / as—
ORLOK: Hello Tom.
TOM: Fuck! Oh Jesus Christ / I—

TOM drops the phone.

ORLOK: I've startled you.
TOM: Sorry. I didn't see you.

TOM picks the phone up. Sees it's hung up.

Shit. Sorry. I'm yes I'm Tom. You / must be—
ORLOK: Count Orlok.

ORLOK puts his hand out. TOM *takes it.*

TOM: Sorry it's so late wow you've got / cold hands.
ORLOK: It's not late.

TOM: It's after / midnight

ORLOK: You must be hungry. Come in.

The door to the house materialises.

TOM: God, the door's right there. I could / have sworn …

The door opens. ORLOK *motions inside.*

ORLOK: Please, enter freely and of your own will.

> TOM *hesitates, then goes through the door into a grand, cavernous room. A table is laid with food. Far more food than one person could ever eat.*

The servants are asleep / now but they

TOM: Servants?

ORLOK: prepared you something. Eat. Drink.

> TOM *starts putting food on his plate.* ORLOK *watches. Through the following* ORLOK *passes* TOM *plates of food, encouraging him to eat.*

TOM: You're not eating?

ORLOK: I'm practising self-restraint. You've been to the land of thieves and phantoms before?

TOM: The … ?

ORLOK: Sydney.

TOM: Oh. Yes, a couple of times. Thank you for agreeing to / meet with me.

ORLOK: Do you play with your food, Tom?

TOM: … No?

ORLOK: I do. Nasty habit.

TOM:

ORLOK: So. Tell me about Bluewater.

TOM: Of course. It's … a great place. We really / think it has a lot of

ORLOK: The name?

TOM: There's a small lake, the tarn. It's …

ORLOK: Blue?

TOM: Right.

ORLOK: I like small towns.

TOM: It has a lot of potential. We think there's opportunity / in many different industries

ORLOK: Not to live, but to visit.

TOM: Tourism is definitely an untapped / market.

ORLOK: You like the house?

TOM: Yes, it's … big.

ORLOK: How embarrassing.

TOM: Is it just you?

ORLOK: It is now.

    Beat.

TOM: How long have you lived here?

ORLOK: Hundred, hundred and fifty years.

TOM: Your family?

ORLOK: You want to know how I choose my investments. It's very simple. I hear of places, people in need. I write to them, offer them money, invite them into my home.

TOM: How did you hear about us?

ORLOK: I have certain … networks.

TOM: Like, philanthropic / … ?

ORLOK: Do you like fishing?

TOM: Fishing? I … It's okay.

ORLOK: Doesn't quite have the thrill of the hunt. But there is a certain joy in waiting to see what you can reel in. Philanthropically speaking.

TOM: It's very generous.

ORLOK: You've always lived in Bluewater?

TOM: Mostly. Melbourne for a few years, but.

ORLOK: What drew you back?

TOM: I wanted to be closer to my family.

ORLOK: There are others like you?

TOM: Others?

ORLOK: Brothers, sisters.

TOM: Just my parents. I had a younger brother. There was a collapse at the mine / and he (died)

ORLOK: I've experienced death myself.

TOM: I'm sorry.

ORLOK: We turn to our work, don't we?

TOM: / Yes.

ORLOK: I've been on something of a sabbatical, but I do love my calling. The drive for more, for better. The hunger.

TOM: You're … ambitious.

ORLOK: I've been hoping to expand my family.

TOM: You have / children?

ORLOK: An apprentice. Someone ruthless, insatiable, someone ambitious, like you say. Who not only craves more but yearns for it. You're not like that.

TOM: Well, I …

ORLOK: It wasn't a question.

    The right person just refuses to present themselves.

TOM: There's a skills shortage.

ORLOK: Isn't there?

    What about the earth? In Bluewater.

TOM: The … landscape?

ORLOK: The soil, Tom. Keep up.

TOM: Sorry, yes … the land isn't suitable for agriculture. Right now. But we think with / time that

ORLOK: So nothing grows.

TOM: Not nothing. We've just discovered a species of iris has adapted to eat insects so / we think

ORLOK: A carnivore.

TOM: Right. So we think that with some time / and investment it could be

ORLOK: These trees weren't always here. I planted them.

TOM: / You … ?

ORLOK: I like to be in the forest. Reminds me of home.

TOM: Where are / you … ?

ORLOK: My earth is very special. Very strong. Have you ever stood on a battlefield?

TOM: … I uh … No.

ORLOK: I have. I've commanded armies. Men have died here.

TOM: Are you / talking about … (frontier wars)?

ORLOK: This land is enriched with their blood.

TOM: You can't say that.

ORLOK: You have a soldier's heart.

TOM: I … do?

ORLOK: The land must be fed, you can't just take from it. Do you see?
TOM: Of / course, I …
ORLOK: You're desperate.
TOM: I wouldn't / say that we're
ORLOK: You'd do anything. To save the town.
TOM: I … Yes. I would.

> *Beat.*

ORLOK: No more business tonight. Try the bread, it's very fresh.
TOM: If you have any more questions, I …
ORLOK: It's time to eat.
TOM: I have to leave, in the morning, so …
ORLOK: You'll stay.
TOM: Tonight, of course.
ORLOK: A week or so.
TOM: A week?
ORLOK: Or so.
TOM: / No I …
ORLOK: You should write to your girlfriend, tell her you'll be delayed.
TOM: I really can't / stay that long.
ORLOK: I have a pen and paper here.
TOM: Did I say / that I had a (girlfriend)?
ORLOK: Tell her you love her. Eat the bread.

> ORLOK *passes* TOM *a knife.* TOM *blindly takes it and starts cutting a slice of bread.*

All this business. I'm famished.

> TOM *cuts his hand with the knife. It's bleeding.*

TOM: Shit.
ORLOK: Your blood.

> TOM *picks up a napkin and goes to wipe the blood away.* ORLOK *rushes to him and grabs his hand. He moves quicker than seems possible.*

Don't waste it!

> TOM *freezes.* ORLOK *licks the blood from* TOM*'s hand.*

SCENE SEVEN

The next morning. ELLEN *wakes from a nightmare, on the sofa. She sits bolt upright and shouts out.* KATE *is there. There's a box of books somewhere, and* ELLEN*'s demon book.*

KATE: It's okay.
ELLEN: … What?
KATE: You're awake.
ELLEN: / Who … ?
KATE: It's me. It's Kate.
ELLEN: Kate. What are you … ?
KATE: I was at the door.
ELLEN: / I …
KATE: I heard shouting. I knocked but, I just wanted to make sure / that you were alright
ELLEN: No I was just … I just had the weirdest … Kate. Sorry. Hi.
KATE: Hi.
ELLEN: What time is it?
KATE: Just after nine.
ELLEN: I must have slept like … sixteen hours, shit. How / did you … ?
KATE: The door was open.

> ELLEN *picks up her phone. It's dead.*

ELLEN: / Shit.
KATE: I'm not listening at the walls or anything.
ELLEN: No, I didn't think / you were listening …
KATE: Small town. Everyone in each other's business.
ELLEN: It's fine, really.

> ELLEN *finds a charger and plugs her phone in.*

KATE: I thought you were being murdered.
ELLEN: Yeah, no, that's … possible.
KATE: Or Tom was.
ELLEN: Or I was being murdered by Tom. Statistically.
KATE: Right. Exactly.

ELLEN: Well, he's in Sydney. And he'd never have the guts.

> *Beat.*

KATE: I brought books. More. / I thought you might …
ELLEN: Oh yeah great, thanks.

> ELLEN *goes to the box of books.* KATE *picks up the demon book and starts flicking through it.*

KATE: Mum was so into myths and monsters / and all that.
ELLEN: I can't put that one down.
KATE: Is. She is into.
ELLEN: Just find myself holding it.
KATE: I keep doing that.
ELLEN: I've been meaning to go see her.
KATE: It's okay, if / you …

> KATE *finds a page in the book, starts reading it.*

ELLEN: No, she was nice to us, when we moved in. You know people still talk about her.
KATE: I know.
ELLEN: She's kind of amazing.
KATE: Mm.
ELLEN: Like, before her time.
KATE: [*reading*] 'The spell of the nosferatu falls quick as darkness, leaving those under it forever marked … '
ELLEN: I mean, eco warrior in a mining town.
KATE: ' … constricted of sense and breath.'
ELLEN: Bet that sucked for you.
KATE: … It did, yeah.
ELLEN: You're being very practical. Clearing out.
KATE: You think I'm heartless.
ELLEN: I think I live in a house full of stuff Tom's brother is never coming back for.

> *Beat.*

KATE: 'Yet hope remains. Deliverance is possible.'

> ELLEN *takes the book from* KATE.

ELLEN: I've been thinking about your funding problem. I could write it up for you. Put the pressure on. 'Affordable local healthcare: dead on arrival.'

KATE: I asked James already.

ELLEN: Why are you and Knock on first name terms?

KATE: He said there's no money.

ELLEN: So you want to go down without a fight?

KATE: Thought you'd given up on Bluewater.

ELLEN: Still need the inches. And Knock only really acts if you threaten him.

> ELLEN's *phone switches back on, starts beeping messages.*

KATE: Sometimes not even then.

> ELLEN *clocks what* KATE *has said but is distracted by her phone.*

ELLEN: Tom. So cute he still leaves voicemails.

KATE: What's he doing in Sydney?

ELLEN: Saving the town, of course.

KATE: You think we're doomed.

ELLEN: Sometimes it's kinder to let things die.

SCENE EIGHT

Night. ORLOK's *house.* TOM *wakes with a start. He is in a box of dirt. He looks ill and confused. There are marks on his neck and arms that he may or may not notice. He frantically brushes the dirt away.*

There's a sound he can't figure out: his phone is ringing. He gets out of the box. He looks around the room, trying to remember. He finds his phone and answers. His voice is croaky.

TOM: Hello?

ELLEN: Tom?

TOM: … Hey.

ELLEN: Oh my god.

TOM: Sorry, my voice.

ELLEN: Fucking hell. Are you okay? Oh my god. / Thank fuck.

TOM: Yeah, I just woke up. I had the / strangest dream.

ELLEN: Oh fuck Tom, thank god. Jesus, / I've been going out of my …

TOM: God, I feel / like shit.

ELLEN: Where the fuck have you been?!

TOM: … I was asleep.

ELLEN: Asleep?!

TOM: Yeah, it's … it's dark, shit is it night? I thought it was morning.

ELLEN: I've been calling you and calling you.

TOM: Sorry, I must have / slept all day.

ELLEN: Fucking hell I thought you were dead. Why haven't you called me back?

TOM: What? I called last night. I left / a message.

ELLEN: Last night?! No you didn't.

TOM: Saying that I'd arrived.

ELLEN: Arrived? What are you talking about?

TOM: Didn't you get my messages?

ELLEN: Tom.

That was two weeks ago.

Beat.

TOM:

ELLEN: Tom?

TOM:

ELLEN: Are you there?

TOM: I … What? No, I …

ELLEN: What's going on? Where are you?

TOM: I'm … Ellen, I'm in Sydney. I'm at this house, I told you.

ELLEN: Yeah I know where you went and I got your fucking letter but you can't just stop answering your phone. You can't just ignore me for two weeks. I've been going out of my mind.

TOM: What … letter? What do you mean two weeks?

ELLEN: You're scaring me. What's happened to you?

TOM: Is this … ? Are you joking?

ELLEN: Am I (joking) … ? Christ. No I'm not fucking joking! You left two weeks ago. You haven't been answering your phone. No-one's heard from you. Not your friends, not your parents. Then a week ago I get this letter saying you don't know when you're going to be back, like you can just leave and tell me by fucking post. And I've been calling and calling and Knock's been trying to find you but he lost the fucking address and

I called the police but they basically laughed me out because I have this ridiculous fucking letter and it's in your handwriting so everything must be fine like it's the eighteenth fucking century. And I kept thinking that you'd been murdered or abducted or fucking brainwashed or or or you'd just run away and I'd never see you again. Can you just tell me what's going on? Can you just come home?

While ELLEN *talks,* TOM *looks around the room. There are two or more doors. He tries them all—they're locked. He gets increasingly frantic.*

A door opens behind TOM *and* ORLOK *appears in the doorway, in shadow.* TOM *freezes.*

Tom? Tom?

TOM: I have to go.

ELLEN: What? No, I—

He hangs up, but keeps his back to ORLOK.

ORLOK: You're awake.

TOM: What's happening?

ORLOK: It's good to see you up and about. You seem better.

TOM: Have I been sick?

ORLOK: A little.

TOM: How long have I—

TOM turns as ORLOK *steps into the light of the room. He looks noticeably younger—less grey, straight-backed, handsome even.* TOM *stops short.*

Your face.

You look … You look …

ORLOK: Yes?

TOM: Young.

ORLOK: Your visit has been most refreshing.

The sound of a baby crying.

TOM: What have you done to me?

ORLOK: I have given you food, a roof, a bed.

TOM: That sound.

ORLOK: There's no sound.

TOM: Why am I still here?
ORLOK: I thought we were having fun.
TOM: The doors are locked.
ORLOK: Safety.

The crying gets louder.

TOM: You can't hear that?
ORLOK: Don't get distracted. You're awake. You seem much better.
TOM: Have I been sick?
ORLOK: A little.
TOM: I don't remember.
ORLOK: Tell me what you want.
TOM: Please, that sound, you can't hear it?
ORLOK: Tom. There is. No sound.

The crying stops.

TOM: How long have I been here?
ORLOK: I thought you were improving.
TOM: Have I been sick?
ORLOK: Extremely.
TOM: The doors are locked.
ORLOK: Security.
TOM: I have to go somewhere.
ORLOK: Ah! Interesting. Go on.

A wolf howls.

TOM: What was that?
ORLOK: Don't get distracted.
TOM: How long have I been here?
ORLOK: She told you. On the phone.
TOM: That's not … possible.
ORLOK: She's been so worried about you.
TOM: Are you keeping me?
ORLOK: You're keeping yourself.
TOM: How did I get here?
ORLOK: You were lost.
TOM: You took me in.
ORLOK: We've been so good for each other.

TOM: I wanted something.

ORLOK: That's right.

TOM: The land.

ORLOK: Very good. What else?

TOM: Was that a wolf?

ORLOK: Concentrate.

TOM: It's not possible.

ORLOK: You must stop this obsession with possibility.

TOM: Why am I still here? Have I been sick?

ORLOK: Remember. The woman on the phone.

TOM: The phone?

ORLOK: Back in the box!

> TOM *stops and for a second, he might resist. Then he dutifully gets back in the box of dirt.*

> ORLOK *has* TOM*'s phone, he's scrolling through it.*

Ellen has been calling so much.

TOM: How / did you … ?

ORLOK: She's wondered why, if you're dead, your phone has stayed on. I charged it for you, I hope you don't mind. It's a little game I like to play. She sounded so upset in her messages. But angry, too. Furious. I like that.

   And she seems to like you. They all do, the people who've called. So I've been thinking that perhaps it should be you that introduces me.

TOM: I have to leave.

ORLOK: So you agree.

TOM: What's happening?

ORLOK: You're awake you've been a little sick but you're better now it's been two weeks you fell ill but I've cared for you you're very grateful perhaps you would even call us friends it was a dream that's all a nightmare there's somewhere you need to be.

TOM: The doors are locked.

ORLOK: No. They're not.

> *Maybe* TOM *tries the door and it opens, or* ORLOK *opens it.*

TOM: I thought you were keeping me.

ORLOK: You're my guest. I believe in observing the formalities, don't you?

TOM: I have to go home.

ORLOK: Exactly. And where's that?

TOM: Ellen.

ORLOK: That's not a location.

TOM: There's a town. An island.

ORLOK: Which is it?

TOM: Bluewater.

ORLOK: Tell me what you want.

TOM: I want to go home.

ORLOK: And?!

TOM: And take you with me.

ORLOK: Finally. An invitation.

SCENE NINE

Radio calls:

CAPTAIN: Passage log for ship *Empusa*. Sailing Port Jackson Bay to Macquarie Harbour. Private charter, two passengers plus cargo, nine crew including myself. Clear conditions expected.

Hello all stations, hello all stations.

This is the *Empusa*, victor hotel quebec two seven three nine.

Position: Three six degrees, two two minutes, two three decimal eight south. One five two degrees, four nine minutes, five seven decimal four east.

Severe weather warning for all vessels. Sudden dense fog. Visibility: very poor. Repeat. Dense fog. Visibility: very poor.

Over.

Urgent call for all stations, urgent call for all stations.

This is the *Empusa*.

Position: three eight degrees, four seven minutes, three five decimal seven south. One five zero degrees, zero seven minutes, zero eight decimal three east.

Passenger missing, suspected overboard. Visibility still very poor. Attempting rescue. Two crew taken sick. They're saying … They're delirious, hallucinating. Unable to navigate these conditions with crew down. Any vessels nearby, call for urgent assistance, urgent assistance.

Mayday, mayday, mayday.

    This is *Empusa*.

    Ship in immediate danger.

    Four crew missing. I don't know what's …

    Position, uh …

    The rest are sick, all of them. Their faces, I …

    Please, send help. There's something. I think there's someone here, I—

    What's … ?

    Oh god. Fuck.

RESPONDER: Mayday response to *Empusa*, victor hotel quebec two seven three nine. Please respond. Over.

    Empusa. Please respond.

    Please respond.

SCENE TEN

Day. TOM *unconscious in hospital.* ELLEN *is pacing.* TOM *wakes with a start.*

TOM: What's happening?

ELLEN: You're awake.

TOM: What? No. / No no.

ELLEN: Hey. It's okay.

TOM: Let me go.

ELLEN: Lie down. You're okay.

TOM: Dirt. There's dirt. I'm / choking I

ELLEN: What? Dirt?

TOM: / Orlok.

ELLEN: Tom. It's me. / It's me.

TOM: Let me / go.

ELLEN: It's me. It's Ellen.

TOM: Ellen?

ELLEN: Yes. Yes, it's okay.

TOM: Where am I?

ELLEN: You're in hospital. / You're okay.

TOM: Where's Orlok? / Is he here?

ELLEN: Orlok? I … I don't know. He's … No, he's not here.

TOM: The door's locked.

ELLEN: No, it's …

TOM: Why's it closed?

ELLEN: Just for privacy. I / can …

TOM: Open it.

ELLEN: Okay. Okay. It's okay.

> *She opens the door.*

See? Open.

TOM: I have to go home.

ELLEN: You have to rest. They'll need to keep you in for a day or so / they're not sure

TOM: What's happening?

ELLEN: You were injured. You lost a lot of blood. You've been delirious, but you're okay. I'll get the doctor. They'll want to see you now you're awake.

TOM: Did I say something?

ELLEN: No, not really. Nothing I could understand.

TOM: What did I say? What's happened?

ELLEN: … There was an accident. Do you remember?

TOM: The crew.

ELLEN: Don't worry about that now.

TOM: I didn't see anything. I was in the box.

ELLEN: In the … room? The cabin?

TOM: It's not possible.

ELLEN: The police will want to talk to you when / you're feeling better

TOM: No police.

ELLEN: Not till you're ready.

TOM: Ellen. You're here.

ELLEN: Yes. Yes.

TOM: I'm okay. I had a dream. A nightmare, that's all. I'm ready to go home now.

ELLEN: Not yet.

TOM: I was sick.

> But I seem much better.

SCENE ELEVEN

Day. Kate's clinic. KATE *taking* ELLEN's *blood.*

ELLEN: I just thought, better to be safe.

KATE: If it'll put your mind at rest.

ELLEN: I mean if there's a possibility Tom had some sort of contagious …
/ or …

KATE: What did the tests say?

ELLEN: Inconclusive. I wanted to get tested at the hospital but they
didn't think there was any point / so I just thought

KATE: I'm happy to do it.

ELLEN: I can control this, you know?

KATE: Has he said anything?

ELLEN: I'm practising patience.

KATE: Are you sleeping?

ELLEN: No. He's having these nightmares. Terrors.

KATE: He should speak to someone.

ELLEN: In the day he's … fine. He's being sort of, aggressively fine.
He just feels … far away.

> KATE *marks up the blood sample.*
>
> *Time splits. That night,* KNOCK *enters the clinic.* ORLOK *appears
> in the doorway behind him.*

KNOCK: And this is Doctor Bulwer's clinic. I uh—

> *He turns and sees* ORLOK *hasn't entered.*

Sorry. Come in. Come in.

> ORLOK *crosses the threshold. We see now that he is young and
> radiant.*

This formality. Is it … cultural or … ?

ELLEN: He wants us to eat with him.

ORLOK: In a manner of speaking.

ELLEN: Knock. In our house. He wants us to host this … I mean, break
bread, with this this this boyfriend-stealer, this poisoner, this boat-
taking, New South Wales-living fucking … count.

KATE: James told me.

KNOCK: That's everywhere now.

ORLOK: You've been most welcoming.

KNOCK: It's no trouble. Want to make sure that you're happy, with everything.

ELLEN: I mean, it's a chance to get some answers. Thought I might interview him, for the paper.

KNOCK: It's late. Sorry, of course we'll arrange for accommodation / and

ORLOK: Not necessary.

KNOCK: Really, as a new benefactor we'd / like to

ORLOK: I travel with everything I need.

KATE: James invited me actually, to the dinner.

ELLEN: … Did he?

KNOCK: Well. If there's anything else I can do for you. Anything at all.

KATE: And I heard he refused medical intervention. Orlok.

ELLEN: Can he do that?

KATE: Isn't he a billionaire? They don't exactly play by the rules.

> KATE *puts the blood into cold storage,* ORLOK *takes it straight back out. He reads the name on the sample and smiles.*

KNOCK: Oh, I don't think / we should—

ORLOK: For testing.

> ORLOK *slips the blood into his pocket. He steps closer to* KNOCK.

KNOCK: I'm sure there's a / lab that will

ORLOK: You said anything.

ELLEN: So you're coming? To the dinner?

ORLOK: Though I do hate it cold.

KATE: Could be interesting.

KNOCK: You … ? What?

ELLEN: Perfect, actually. You can be my backup.

KATE: I thought he might have some spare money. For the clinic.

ORLOK: There is one more thing you can do for me.

KNOCK: Whatever you need.

KATE: And I'd love to know what he's got planned.

> ORLOK *bares his teeth.*

SCENE TWELVE

If seeing ORLOK *crossing the threshold into Tom and Ellen's house feels important, put it here.*

Night. Everyone in Tom and Ellen's. All, except ORLOK, *drinking from a case of wine. If there's food, no-one notices* ORLOK *not eating it. Some lines are indicated, but almost any line could be directed at* ORLOK *here, whether it makes sense or not.*

ELLEN: [*to* ORLOK] A winery?

KATE: [*to* ORLOK] Well that's …

KNOCK: [*to* ORLOK] Perfect.

ELLEN: [*to* ORLOK] Unexpected.

KATE: [*to* ORLOK] Nothing can grow here.

TOM: The flytrap can.

KNOCK: Orlok says that's not a problem.

KATE: How could / that not … ?

KNOCK: The dirt's imported.

ELLEN: The what?

TOM: The earth. For the vines.

KNOCK: It's here already.

KATE: That's what's in the crates?

ELLEN: [*to* ORLOK] Why here?

KNOCK: Tom made a very convincing case.

TOM: I just said Bluewater was an untapped resource.

KNOCK: We have been more of a beer town, but change: change is good.

KATE: [*to* ORLOK] But why not choose somewhere with fertile ground? Importing your own soil is …

ELLEN: Capitalism on steroids?

KNOCK: Innovation.

ELLEN: [*to* ORLOK] So that's your business? Wine?

KNOCK: We're the first.

ELLEN: [*to* ORLOK] This case you brought, that's / not … ?

TOM: Just a vintage he thought we'd enjoy.

KNOCK: [*to* ORLOK] It's really nice.

KATE: [*to* ORLOK] So what's the timeline, for the vineyard? Years, / surely.

KNOCK: Quicker than you'd think.

ELLEN: [*to* ORLOK] You're not drinking.

KNOCK: He doesn't.

TOM: Orlok really wants to get to know the town. The people.

ELLEN: I'll have to interview you, for the paper.

TOM: Get under our skin.

KNOCK: A homecooked meal was his suggestion.

TOM: Local flavour.

ELLEN: [*to* ORLOK] Did you know there's nothing about you / on the internet?

TOM: This wine really is good.

KNOCK: / [*to* TOM] Isn't it?

ELLEN: [*to* ORLOK] Not even a photo / and Tom couldn't describe you.

TOM: It's rich, and something else ...

KNOCK: There's that ... / taste.

ELLEN: [*to* ORLOK] I mean you think billionaire / you think ... (Bezos?) But you're ... (young? handsome?)

TOM: What do they call that? That sort of aftertaste.

KATE: [*to* TOM] Tannins.

TOM: / Right.

ELLEN: [*to* ORLOK] I'm just trying to get some background.

KNOCK: You need a top up, Ellen?

ELLEN: [*to* ORLOK] Where are you even from?

TOM: Europe, mainly.

ELLEN: [*to* ORLOK] I suppose I should thank you. For looking after Tom, in Sydney.

KNOCK: [*to* ORLOK] We're all so grateful.

KATE: [*to* TOM] How are you feeling?

TOM: [*to* KATE] Fine. Good. [*To* ORLOK] Great.

ELLEN: [*to* ORLOK] Kind of weird you didn't call his family, or ...

KNOCK: He wrote.

ELLEN: [*to* ORLOK] Yes, that wasn't alarming at all.

KNOCK: I'm sure Orlok was very busy.

TOM: The food's almost ready, so ...

KNOCK: [*to* ORLOK] We're just grateful that Tom is okay.

TOM: [*to* ORLOK] There's isn't anything you don't eat, / is there?

ELLEN: [*to* ORLOK] What happened on the boat?

KNOCK: I don't think we need / to …

TOM: [*to* ELLEN] I told you. I was sick. I don't remember.

ELLEN: Orlok wasn't sick.

KNOCK: It was traumatic for everyone.

ELLEN: [*to* ORLOK] Is it true what the police are saying? The men were delirious?

KNOCK: I'm sure none of us want / to talk about it.

ELLEN: [*to* ORLOK] They threw themselves overboard?

TOM: It was me, okay? I was sick. And whatever I had I brought it on to the boat. I put those people in danger. I made them sick and they're dead now. They're dead and it's my fault. So can you just fucking drop it?

> *Beat.*

ELLEN: Your results came back clear.

KNOCK: It was a terrible accident.

KATE: Ellen said it's with the police in Hobart now, so the / investigation should

KNOCK: Exactly, it's out of our hands.

TOM: I hope everyone's hungry.

KNOCK: Starving.

ELLEN: [*to* ORLOK] Okay last thing but—who takes a boat from Sydney?

> KNOCK *and* TOM *both go to speak, but* ORLOK *holds up his hand to stop them.*

ORLOK: If I wanted to fly, I would simply do so.

> *Beat.*

TOM: Let's eat.

> *Time jumps.*

KNOCK: This is delicious.

KATE: Really.

ELLEN: [*to* ORLOK] Have you had some?

KNOCK: [*to* ORLOK] Try these.

TOM: [*to* ORLOK] Have more.

KNOCK: [*to* ORLOK] I'll cut you some.

TOM: [*to* ORLOK] There's salt if you …

ELLEN: [*to* ORLOK] Put the sauce on it.

> *Time jumps.*

ORLOK: There's no church here.

KNOCK: Is that a problem?

TOM: There never was one.

KATE: That is strange, isn't it? I never thought about it.

KNOCK: Industry was focused on the mine. I suppose no-one was
particularly religious.

ELLEN: Even back then?

ORLOK: You're a godless people.

ELLEN: [*to* ORLOK] Is that your preference?

KNOCK: [*to* ORLOK] Smart thinking though. For the winery. Religious
opposition.

ELLEN: Not Christians. Christians are all about wine. It's practically a …

KATE: Transubstantiation.

KNOCK: What?

ELLEN: You know. Bread into flesh. Wine into—

> *Time jumps.*

KATE: How do you get the meat so … ?

TOM: Thighs are easy.

KNOCK: I'm useless.

KATE: No you're not.

TOM: All the flavour's in the fat.

ELLEN: And the bone.

KNOCK: That salt.

KATE: But sweet too.

ELLEN: Really melts in your—

> *Time jumps.*

KNOCK: Bodies. Just writhing around.

TOM: Thousands of them.

KATE: In the soil?

ORLOK: The dirt.

KATE: Well not dirt, obviously.

TOM: It's an ecosystem. Microbes / and …

ELLEN: [*to* ORLOK] So that's how it works, with the vines? The regeneration / or …

KNOCK: The bodies, yes.

KATE: Dirt is dead, only soil is alive. That's the point.

KNOCK: [*to* ORLOK] Kate's really smart with this stuff.

KATE: No, it's just / interesting …

TOM: The new enriches the old.

ELLEN: [*to* ORLOK] Not chemicals?

ORLOK: All organic.

KNOCK: It's their gases, their shit and juices.

TOM: Rewilding. Leaving nature to its own devices so it restores itself.

ORLOK: Removing human intervention.

TOM: Overseas they've reintroduced species that haven't been seen in generations. Wolves in Scotland. Bison in Romania.

KATE: Yes but that takes generations, it's not some quick fix.

TOM: They're bringing the tiger back.

ELLEN: [*to* ORLOK] I wrote about it, for the paper.

KNOCK: It's brilliant.

ELLEN: 'Resurrection of an apex predator.'

KATE: What could possibly go wrong?

> *Time jumps.*

TOM: Beetroot makes it purple.

KNOCK: What's the one with pee?

KATE: Asparagus.

ELLEN: Makes it stink.

TOM: I've heard that, but I've never smelt it.

ELLEN: You've got to get down there.

TOM: There's something about pineapple.

KATE: That's not pee.

> *Time jumps.*

KNOCK: [*to* ORLOK] You have to see it for yourself. It's …

TOM: Sky blue.

ELLEN: Not sky.

TOM: Aquamarine.

ELLEN: Cobalt.

KATE: Stop.

KNOCK: Petrol.

TOM: Opal?

ELLEN: Azure.

KNOCK: It's remarkable.

KATE: [*to* ORLOK] It's the copper.

KNOCK: Kate.

KATE: It's not blue because it's clear. It's not some natural beauty. Maybe a century ago, when the town was built but now it's copper deposits that have leached into the water from the mine. It doesn't just look blue, it really is dyed, glowing, toxic blue.

ORLOK: It's a self-fulfilling prophecy.

KATE: It's a lie.

KNOCK: [*to* ORLOK] A lie that brings the tourists.

ELLEN: [*to* ORLOK] Sometimes a lie is easier.

KATE: [*to* ORLOK] You should know what you're getting into.

> *Time jumps.*

TOM: Hard to describe.

ELLEN: It kind of … bursts?

KATE: Umami.

KNOCK: Have you ever eaten tongue?

> *Time jumps.*

ELLEN: [*to* ORLOK] Mostly obituaries. It's thrilling.

TOM: Your obituaries are the only proof any of us existed.

KNOCK: A local paper is a wonderful thing.

ELLEN: [*to* ORLOK] It is the way I do it.

TOM: A dying art.

ELLEN: [*to* ORLOK] You should read it. If you want to learn about the town. I try to inject a little personality into it.

ORLOK: What about the truth?

ELLEN: I report the facts.

TOM: [*to* ORLOK] She does play both sides though.

ELLEN: [*to* ORLOK] Within the lines.

TOM: [*to* ORLOK] Riles things up.

ELLEN: [*to* ORLOK] Sometimes the right story doesn't just present itself. You have to pursue it. Hunt it down. It's like with interviews.

Profiles. People want to tell you everything. You just have to give them the right encouragement.

ORLOK: And how do you do that?

ELLEN: I make them feel like they can trust me.

ORLOK: So you're ruthless.

ELLEN: People just love to throw themselves on my mercy.

ORLOK: Prove it.

Time jumps.

KATE: They're a little bitter, at the skin.

ELLEN: You have to bite it.

KATE: But sweet, on the inside

TOM: Round and soft.

ELLEN: Pry it open.

TOM: Use your fingers.

ELLEN: Better with your mouth.

Time jumps.

KATE: It's her lungs.

ORLOK: I hear she's a pillar of the community.

KATE: How have you heard that?

ELLEN: [*to* ORLOK] She's a town legend.

KNOCK: [*to* ORLOK] Practically famous.

TOM: [*to* ORLOK] More like infamous.

KNOCK: [*to* ORLOK] She's a great speaker. Almost had me convinced the mine was evil.

ORLOK: You preferred money.

KATE: It's more complicated than that.

KNOCK: It was my dad worked everyone up. [*To* ORLOK] Head of the union.

KATE: [*to* ORLOK] They hated each other. We couldn't even tell them that we were …

ELLEN: I fucking knew / it!

KNOCK: You did, I was the / one that

ELLEN: [*to* TOM] Fifty bucks please.

TOM: [*to* KATE? *Or maybe* ORLOK?] I never took that bet.

KATE: She pissed a lot of people off.

KNOCK: [*to* ORLOK] We're different now. Strong community.

ORLOK: She wasn't afraid to speak an unpopular truth.
KATE: No. She wasn't. / Isn't.
ORLOK: Would you say you're like that?
KATE: Maybe more than I'd like.
ORLOK: You'll carry that on? After she's dead.

    Time jumps.

TOM: [*to* ORLOK] All the guts and eyes and grisly parts.
ELLEN: [*to* ORLOK] The bones are the best bit.
TOM: Suck the marrow out.
KNOCK: / [*to* ORLOK] Have you eaten enough?
ELLEN: [*to* ORLOK] We had this bird.
TOM: [*to* ORLOK] Fowl? Of some kind.
KNOCK: / [*to* ORLOK] Have you drunk enough?
ELLEN: [*to* ORLOK] Skewered hearts.
KNOCK: / [*to* ORLOK] Would you like more of anything?
TOM: [*to* ORLOK] Four hearts. Three wings.
KATE: A strange beast.
KNOCK: / [*to* ORLOK] Is there anything I can get you?
ELLEN: [*to* ORLOK] Tasted amazing.
TOM: [*to* ORLOK] Kind of tough.
KNOCK: / [*to* ORLOK] It's really no trouble.
ELLEN: [*to* ORLOK] Metallic.
TOM: [*to* ORLOK] But worth it.

    Time jumps.

KNOCK: [*to* ORLOK] They could still exist.
KATE: Without the science?
KNOCK: [*to* ORLOK] Out there. In the forests.
TOM: [*to* ORLOK] My dad saw one. He'd stake his life on it.
ELLEN: [*to* ORLOK] I get people writing in. Saying they've seen them.
KATE: [*to* ORLOK] We killed every last one of them.

    From here, KATE *and* ELLEN's *exchange should overlap completely with* KNOCK *and* TOM's, *so we only hear snippets:*

ELLEN: / Obviously hunting's barbaric.
KNOCK: / You believe in things like that?
KATE: / My dad used to shoot, before the buyback.

TOM: / If someone found one now, I don't think I'd believe it.

ELLEN: / Tigers?

KATE: / Smaller. Rabbits?

KNOCK: / That's proof though, isn't it?

ELLEN: / I suppose pest control is different.

TOM: / They used to think the platypus wasn't real, when they brought the bodies back.

KATE: / But we invited the pests in.

KNOCK: / So?

ELLEN: / And you shouldn't kill your guests?

TOM: / So just because something's true, doesn't make it believable.

KATE: Ideally.

The following is heard distinctly:

ELLEN: Size though. Is smaller better?

TOM: For what?

ELLEN: [*to* ORLOK] We're deciding what to kill.

KNOCK: [*to* ORLOK] It's fur for me. Birds are okay. If I had to pick an order.

KATE: I just couldn't do it.

ELLEN: [*to* ORLOK] I think, under the right circumstances …

TOM: It's got to be pain, hasn't it? The ones that feel pain.

KATE: All animals feel fear.

Then complete overlap:

ELLEN: / So if there was a wallaby.

KATE: / No.

KNOCK: / What about monsters?

ELLEN: / You're not vegan. Not even vegetarian.

TOM: / [*to* ORLOK] I probably couldn't kill a monster. They'd be stronger than me for a start.

KATE: / That's not the same.

KNOCK: / I mean believing.

ELLEN: / But you're not innocent.

TOM: / [*to* ORLOK] Monsters are just stories.

KATE: / So you would?

KNOCK: / [*to* ORLOK] But someone believed at some point.

TOM: / [*to* ORLOK] Not like a religion.

ELLEN: / [*to* ORLOK] I'm a lot stronger than I look.

KNOCK: / Greek myths?

TOM: / The Loch Ness monster.

KATE: / I hit something with my car once. Felt it thunk. Might have been a baby kangaroo. I didn't stop, is that bad?

KNOCK: / [*to* ORLOK] Makes a place more interesting.

ELLEN: / [*to* ORLOK] That's lucky. An adult would have wrecked the car.

TOM: / [*to* ORLOK] I suppose. Puts you on the map.

KATE: / A baby though.

KNOCK: [*to* ORLOK] Exactly, so there are advantages.

> *The following is heard distinctly:*

ELLEN: [*to* KATE] What about humans? If you were threatened.

KNOCK: [*to* ORLOK] They don't have to be threatening.

TOM: It's too confusing when they look human.

KATE: What's confusing?

TOM: Monsters.

KNOCK: Good and bad.

ELLEN: [*to* ORLOK] Werewolves are the hottest.

TOM: [*to* ORLOK] We're not talking about having sex with them.

ELLEN: Why not?

KATE: We're still on murder.

> *The following three speeches are spoken simultaneously. As they talk, their voices merge, becoming unintelligible sound. Until we hear only what* ORLOK *hears, the blood sliding endlessly round their bodies, their hearts beating.*

> *You can drown out as much of the following text as feels right.*

TOM: / [*to* ORLOK] I read once about, like a philosophical … a suggestion, that governments should store the nuclear codes sewn up inside a person, by their heart. So if the president or whatever wanted to, you know, go nuclear, they'd have to cut the codes out of the person first. Kill the person, to kill the people.

And I was thinking, imagine if you didn't know it was you. But your fate was sealed anyway. They were sewn in at birth and your parents were told it was a heart operation. And you grow up and have a life and children and worry about normal stuff like taxes and your teeth, and then one day: a knock at the door.

ELLEN: / [*to* ORLOK] Everyone knows monsters are just thinly veiled morality tales. Demons, all of that. A way of policing things. Explaining away our hidden wants and desires. Even from ourselves. And scapegoats, of course. For affairs and illegitimate children. All the forbidden fruit. Scapegoat: from the bible, obviously. Original blame machine. Gives you something to fight against, to kill, to hunt down.

Take werewolves. They kill old people and have sex with newlyweds. That's the folklore. But all that really means is the husband claims werewolf attack and the wife gets stoned to death anyway.

KNOCK: [*to* ORLOK] Anyway you don't need to worry about any invasive species around here. This is just a very normal, stable, small town in Tasmania. Down on its luck, admittedly. But the people are good. Honest. We're miners. We know how to do it tough, when we need to. We all just want what's best for Bluewater and if that means a little sacrifice then I'm sure everyone understands.

But I think you've won them over tonight. Even Kate. They're very impressed with your vision for the future. And that's all we really want is for the town to survive, to get better, for there to be something more than just existing.

The heartbeats are loud now. Close. Almost too much. It would feel so good to make it stop, to drain all of them right this second. So satisfying. So delicious. Even just one of them would be—

KATE: Is it always like this?

ORLOK's focus snaps to KATE. KNOCK, TOM *and* ELLEN *are still talking, we just can't hear them.*

ORLOK: ?
KATE: Everyone performing for you.
ORLOK: You're not.
KATE: … No.

Time jumps.

ORLOK: I was ten, my first. That was the age. The induction into manhood. It was winter, the last month before I was sent from home. It was always dark, in the forest, but my father was an expert tracker, so it wasn't long until we found the animal. A stag.

I had accompanied the hunt on many occasions, but this was the first time I held the bow in my hands. And I found to my disgrace that I was shaking. I mis-hit, catching it in the side. My father was angry. The animal's pain, its fear—toughens the meat, poisons the blood.

Still, quarry mustn't be wasted. He held it, gave me a knife, and told me to finish what I had started. It wasn't his hunting knife, which was thin and sharp. It was smaller, thicker, a knife he used to mark the trees to keep our path.

The creature struggled, but my father urged me on and I held the blunted blade to its neck.

The most surprising thing about death, to the living, is the heat. You think of the dead as cold, stiff. But at the moment of their death they are hot, supple, pulsating in your hands. More alive than ever.

It looked me in the eye. And I'm ashamed to say I faltered.

Still holding it, my father pushed me to the ground till I was looking up, its head above me. I felt the need to reach out, put my hand to its chest. It was quivering. We both were.

Then in one motion my father took his hunting knife and slashed its throat.

That warm gush of liquid. Over my hand, through my hair, down my face, my lips, the back of my neck.

At the house, my father skinned the beast as I watched and when he was done he wrapped the dripping hide around my shoulders as I cried.

I wore that skin for three days. I can still smell it.

It was a hard lesson, but a valuable one. And I never hesitated to kill again. It's only hesitation that causes suffering. We must respect the thing that feeds us.

Pause

ELLEN: I have so many questions.

TOM: I'm going to be sick.

KNOCK: We're just so grateful that you're here.

ORLOK: A toast. To Bluewater.

ALL: To Bluewater.

ORLOK: My very own bountiful winepress.

Perhaps now there's something red in ORLOK*'s glass. They drink.*

INTERLUDE

Time passes, the town transforms. Vines and flytraps grow, covering the land.

KATE, *as in the Prologue. She reads from* ELLEN'*s book of demons:*

KATE: The spell of the nosferatu falls quick as darkness, leaving those under it forever marked, constricted of sense and breath.

Yet hope remains. Deliverance is possible. But by no other means than an innocent maiden become unholy.

With the vile sacrifice of her own bloode, she alone maketh the nosferatu heed not the rising of the sun.

ACT TWO

SCENE ONE

Night. KNOCK, *in shadow. His arm is held out at a strange angle. And there's a shape we can't quite make out.*

KNOCK: I liked the darkness. The heat, underground. The routine. The one task. The focus. The repetition. The way days had a start and an end. The simplicity, camaraderie. The exhaustion. There was something safe about it. Something reassuring. I knew what I was doing. I knew who I was.

> *The shadow shifts.* ORLOK *raises his head from* KNOCK's *arm. His mouth is covered in blood.*

ORLOK: And now?

KNOCK: Now you're here.

ORLOK: That's right.

> ORLOK *drinks again.*

KNOCK: What was I saying? The opening went very ... No-one could believe the way the vines had grown, the red of the wine. The taste. It's strong, isn't it? Intoxicating.

I'm so hungry.

You can feel it in the air. The difference. It smells ...

People have been thanking me. Congratulating me. Even my dad. I like that.

It's cold. Is the window open?

The Joneses left. The Nguyens. The Colemans. It's like you said, so foolish to leave now. When things are only getting better. It's so clever the way you've ...

You're so clear. So sure. How do you do that?

ORLOK: You've said that.

KNOCK: They delayed the report. A miracle, they said. The scientists. Did I tell you that? They can't understand it. The land. Is the door open?

Tom's working late. He's been working a lot. Have you noticed?

It's just it's just it's just …

Unemployment's the lowest in a decade. Predictions for next quarter are even … We're all free now, we're all

It's not that I mind but, it's not him too, is it?

The interview. Ellen's been asking. I've told her she has to be patient.

Expansion is a wonderful idea. Joe didn't turn up for our meeting. Did I (tell you that?)? Did I?

Tom's working late. Again, again. Ellen calls. She calls, he dodges. I wondered … it isn't … Tom. You're not … It's not that I care. I feel different I … Can you hear that?

Kate says people haven't been showing up for appointments.

Everyone must be feeling better. That's good, isn't it?

It's been so good to see Kate again. She was the one that got away. Did I tell you that? I always thought about her. I've been visiting her mum, just to see her. I want to see her. I want to tell her …

You're so confident. So calm. So certain.

The way they look at you. I wish I could be like that.

ORLOK: You've said that.

KNOCK: If I was more like that. If I'd stood up for myself, for us, maybe Kate would have …

I'm starving, restless, can't sit still

Double production, triple it. We'll need more dirt more dirt more dirt more

Ellen's been

I've been thinking about Tom. It's not that I'm jealous I just want, I just think, it's not that I'm but I thought it was just us. I just want to make sure everyone's okay.

The Khans left their car in the driveway. Did I tell you that? Ellen's been

And all their furniture in the house. The Turners too. She's been asking questions.

I told her, it's like you said. There are new people. The new people replace the old. It's like you said. Just the churn the churn the churn of bodies under capitalism.

You're so persuasive. So powerful. Can you teach me how to be like that?

I want it I want it I … Yes. That's what I want.

ORLOK: You've said that.

KNOCK: Have I? I'm sorry I …

ORLOK: There is a way.

KNOCK: I'm so hungry.

ORLOK: If you want to be like me.

KNOCK: I want that.

ORLOK: And in return?

KNOCK: Anything.

ORLOK: Total loyalty.

KNOCK: Of course. I like that. I like it.

ORLOK: You're mine now, you understand?

KNOCK: I I I I feel cold. Hot. Angry. Everything burns, aches. Is that normal?

ORLOK: That's normal.

KNOCK: Is it close now?

ORLOK: What can you see?

KNOCK: Just spots. Patches. It hurts.

ORLOK: Not for long. Here.

> ORLOK *bites his own wrist and offers his blood to* KNOCK.

KNOCK: That smell.

> KNOCK *drinks gratefully from* ORLOK. *Then greedily.* ORLOK *pulls his arm away.*

ORLOK: That's enough.

> ORLOK *drinks from* KNOCK *again, more viciously.*

KNOCK: And everyone will be safe won't they? I just want … I want that. I want …

> KNOCK *passes out.* ORLOK *keeps drinking, hunched over, until* KNOCK *is drained. This is the first time we see* ORLOK *truly animal. Once* KNOCK *dies,* ORLOK *stands and watches.* KNOCK *lies motionless for a while.*

SCENE TWO starts to encroach: The next night, Lillian Bulwer's palliative care room. And the following morning, KATE *in her clinic, whilst* TOM *paces outside.*

A fly begins to buzz around KNOCK. ORLOK *enters Lillian's room.* TOM *enters the clinic.*

KNOCK *wakes suddenly. He senses the fly. Perhaps smelling it before he hears it. He watches, before plucking it from the air. He considers, then eats it. It tastes good.*

TOM: I'm at home. It's dark and I can feel someone behind me. I want to turn but I can't. I feel them getting closer. A touch on the back of my neck. I'm scared, but something else too. A sort of pain or—

He stops himself saying 'excitement'.

anticipation.

ORLOK *draws the curtain around Lillian's bed. We see his shadow approach—the Nosferatu silhouette. He attacks. Blood spurts up on the curtain.*

It must be cold because I can see my breath, but it doesn't disappear, it's like smoke, filling the room. And a sound: running water. Or or someone laughing. This cruel laugh. And this smell, like … earth. Dirt.

Then all of a sudden there's a rush and everything is warm and bright, the air is almost liquid, thick and shiny, and I feel calm and light and content like I'm floating.

But then it turns bitter. Dread. A cold hand gripping. And I panic and I try to fight against it but it pushes me back. And that thick air starts pouring down my throat till I'm choking and I can't breathe and …

I don't think it's a dream.

I think it might be … real.

Beat.

KATE: It's always the same?

TOM: Always.

KATE: Tom, what happened to you—When someone survives a traumatic incident / they can start to feel

TOM: No no it's not that. It's not that. You don't understand. When I wake up I have these marks. These bruises.

KATE: / Bruises?

TOM: And I can feel him. He's right there. He's right behind me.

KATE: Who's behind you?

SCENE THREE starts to encroach: That night. ORLOK *and* ELLEN *outside the mayor's office.*

Through the next three lines, KATE*'s mobile rings.*

ELLEN: I said I was researching a novel.

ORLOK: And they believed that?

ELLEN: They were naïve.

KATE: Sorry. Sorry, I'll turn it off.

TOM: I should go.

KATE: No, it's just my mum's home, I'll call them back.

ELLEN: And I was fresh out of uni, they probably thought I was harmless.

ORLOK: That was naïve.

> TOM *is leaving.*

KATE: Wait, Tom.

TOM: I shouldn't have come.

KATE: What bruises? Who's behind you?

TOM: Please. Don't tell.

> TOM *exits.* KATE *exits through the following.*

ELLEN: Someone showed me round. They liked their work. They were nice to me. They thought I didn't see it. The beating. There was this yard, I snuck out. Filmed the whole thing. We got it shut down.

ORLOK: Did you feel bad?

ELLEN: Only for the animals.

ORLOK: The killing.

ELLEN: The torture.

ORLOK: You still think about it.

ELLEN: Of course. It was my big break.

ORLOK:

ELLEN: Inside, it was split into two long rooms. At the start of the first room was a live cow. And everything in that room was recognisably, you know, animal. Legs and head and skin. But through the door, in the second room, it was just … meat. Different cuts, different quality. But the strange thing … The eeriest thing was …

That story you told. About the deer. Was that true?

ORLOK: You know it was.

ELLEN: I'm meeting Tom. Is he here?

ORLOK: He left.
ELLEN: When?
ORLOK: I'm not his keeper.
ELLEN: Then I should go.
ORLOK: You should.

> *She gets out a packet of cigarettes and takes one out.*

ELLEN: He hates me smoking. I told him I quit.

> *She offers one to* ORLOK. *He refuses. She goes to light hers, but the lighter only sparks. She tries a few more times. Nothing. Eventually,* ORLOK *silently holds his hand out.* ELLEN *passes him the lighter. He tries it, it flames first time. She lights up, then silently takes the lighter back and puts it away.*

Did you hear about Lillian?
ORLOK: I did.
ELLEN: That's the fourth missing person. Officially. But my count is closer to fifteen, twenty. If you include the families who've left, the tourists running out on their / hotel bills.
ORLOK: I read your front page. Very sensational.
ELLEN: People have been slow, reporting the disappearances. You know, it's a drunk, a wayward teenager, people who were always talking about leaving. I've been asking Knock about it. What he's doing to keep people safe. He won't make a statement. Now he's stopped even answering my calls. It's like I'm the only one taking it seriously.
ORLOK: They're lucky to have you.
ELLEN: There was blood at the scene. Lillian.
ORLOK: Careless.
ELLEN: He's getting sloppy. Could be a game changer, for the story. I think I'll catch him before the cops do.
ORLOK: You think … a man?
ELLEN: I think it's the only explanation.
ORLOK: That's absurd.
ELLEN: Why?
ORLOK: No man would be clever enough, quick enough, strong enough.
ELLEN: To kill?
ORLOK: To get away with it.

She gets her phone out.

ELLEN: Would you like to comment, for the paper? People dropping like flies. You must be worried about your investment.

ORLOK: I don't worry.

ELLEN: You've been avoiding me. Our interview.

ORLOK: You're not ready.

ELLEN: For what?

ORLOK: Tell me the eeriest thing.

ELLEN: ?

ORLOK: At the abattoir.

ELLEN: … The meat.

In the second room. At the end, there was a machine, plastic packaging. The blood and fat all vacuum sealed, sanitised. I picked one up. Like the supermarket.

ORLOK: I see.

ELLEN: But the strange thing. The eerie thing was, it was …

ORLOK: Yes.

ELLEN: Hot. Still hot.

ORLOK: Still alive.

ELLEN: Exactly like you said.

ORLOK: You can't stop thinking about it.

ELLEN: No.

ORLOK: You want to feel it again.

ELLEN: I …

Perhaps they are very close now. Almost touching.

Then ORLOK *breaks the spell.*

ORLOK: Tom will be waiting.

ELLEN: … Yes.

SCENE FOUR starts to encroach: Later that night. ORLOK *and* TOM *in Tom and Ellen's bedroom.* TOM *holds the book of demons. He has his back to* ORLOK.

TOM: 'Such is the rapture of the nosferatu that even the strongest man may submit.'

ORLOK: Funny that he left, when you'd arranged to meet here.

ELLEN: Maybe he forgot.

> ELLEN *stubs out her cigarette.*

TOM: 'But a weak man succumbs not only to the draining of his veins ...

ORLOK: You know it's very bad for you.

ELLEN: Smoking?

ORLOK: Lying.

TOM: ' ... but to suckling himself on the bloode of the beaste.'

> ELLEN *exits.* ORLOK *takes the book from* TOM. *Perhaps they read a few words together.*

ORLOK: 'A terrible exchange that surrenders all his days to the night.'

> ORLOK *closes the book.*

So. Would you like to go first, or shall I?

TOM: Is this how it starts?

ORLOK: The terrible exchange.

TOM: What are you doing here?

ORLOK: I'm going to make you submit.

TOM: Who are you?

ORLOK: Call me ... Mayor? No ...

TOM: / Ellen ...

ORLOK: Call me Count.

> TOM *faces* ORLOK *for the first time.*

TOM: Count. You can't be here.

ORLOK: Yet here I am. Tall, charming, mainly from Europe. Are you ready to surrender?

TOM: Ellen will be home any minute.

ORLOK: No, she won't.

TOM: Have you done something to her?

ORLOK: You'd like that, wouldn't you?

TOM: No, / I ...

ORLOK: Yes, you would.

TOM: Yes. I would.

ORLOK: Get her out of the way.

TOM: She can never know about this.

ORLOK: I can keep a secret.

TOM: Are you ... keeping me?

ORLOK: Tell me you're scared.

TOM: I'm … scared.

ORLOK: Terrified. Helpless. Dreading what I might do to you.

TOM: What are you going to do to me?

ORLOK: The weak man.

TOM: I'll do whatever you want. I'll submit.

ORLOK: We don't have long.

TOM: We don't?

ORLOK: Haven't you read the papers? The world's ending.

> *Beat. They're very close now.*

TOM: If I'm the weak man. What does that make you?

ORLOK: Isn't it obvious?

> TOM *kisses* ORLOK.

> *A moment, where we're not sure how* ORLOK *will react.*

> *Then they kiss, things escalate,* ORLOK *pins* TOM *down.*

ORLOK: Tell me what you want.

TOM: I want to succumb to you.

ORLOK: What else?

TOM: I want you to bite me.

ORLOK: Call me Count.

TOM: I want you to bite me, again, Count. Laugh at me. Choke me. Suck my blood.

> *As* ORLOK *bites him,* TOM *closes his eyes. When he opens them, it isn't* ORLOK, *it's* ELLEN.

TOM: … Ellen!

> ELLEN *carries on as though nothing's changed because, for her, it hasn't.*

ELLEN: I said: Call me Count.

TOM: … What's happening?

ELLEN: What? What's wrong?

TOM: Ellen. Fuck.

> TOM *gets up, away from her. As far as possible.*

ELLEN: Tom, what is it?

TOM: Oh my / god.

ELLEN: What just / happened?

TOM: What no nothing. / Nothing.

ELLEN: Was it … too much?

TOM: No, / I …

ELLEN: I thought you liked it.

TOM: Yeah I I I I / did I, shit

ELLEN: You're freaking out.

TOM: I'm not. I'm fine.

ELLEN: If you didn't … (like it) you just needed to tell me.

TOM: No. I did. I do. Let's … let's carry on. I'm fine.

ELLEN: Are you kidding? You just ran away.

TOM: Yeah. No. I might, I might go for a walk / or …

ELLEN: Well you can't leave, we should talk about what just / happened

TOM: I have to go to work.

ELLEN: / What?

TOM: I have, there's something, I've just realised, remembered, something / so I have to

ELLEN: You're going to work? / Now?

TOM: The Count—Orlok just asked me to do something for / him so I have to

ELLEN: It's the middle of the night.

TOM: No yeah that's when Orlok's normally in / anyway so

ELLEN: What? / Why?

TOM: He's kind of … nocturnal / so

ELLEN: Whatever look I thought we were, we were having fun, finally actually connecting and then suddenly you're just back / on another fucking planet.

TOM: I'm fine there's just this stuff Orlok really / needs me to do so

ELLEN: Can you stop talking about Orlok?

TOM: I'm not.

ELLEN: Yes you are.

TOM: It's just work / so I don't know why you'd

ELLEN: I mean, he's literally all you ever / talk about

TOM: / No he's not …

ELLEN: Orlok said / this

TOM: / I barely ever …

ELLEN: Orlok did / that

TOM: / That's ridiculous …

ELLEN: Orlok Orlok thinks, / wants, needs

TOM: / I don't know what you're …

ELLEN: What are you, in love with him?

TOM:

ELLEN:

TOM: No, I …

ELLEN: … Oh my god.

TOM: No, no no, Ellen …

ELLEN: I was joking.

TOM: I know. It's a joke. That would be completely … / absurd so

ELLEN: What the fuck?

TOM: No, it's not / like that I

ELLEN: Has something happened?

TOM: No, you were the / one who

ELLEN: Were you just thinking about him?

TOM: (well, yes, but … weren't you?)

ELLEN: / Fuck.

TOM: You were the one who, who started this, this … whatever this is. Was.

ELLEN: I started it?

TOM: Yes. The book.

ELLEN: You were pretty fucking into it.

TOM: It's not like that.

ELLEN: What's it like?

TOM: I would never.

ELLEN: Never what?

TOM: Me and and Orlok / I

ELLEN: Why not?

TOM: What?

ELLEN: Why not? He's rich, successful, young, hot, / charismatic

TOM: He's not young.

ELLEN: I'd totally fuck him.

TOM: / You'd …

ELLEN: / What?

TOM: You'd 'totally fuck him?' / Are you jealous of me or him?

ELLEN: What do you mean he's / not young?

TOM: You have, you've felt it too.

ELLEN: Felt what?

TOM: The way he

How he makes you

The way he … is. To be with, to be around

ELLEN: I don't know what you're talking about.

TOM: You want something to have happened. To blow things up. To fuck everything.

ELLEN: It was just a game.

TOM: You were pretending to be him.

ELLEN: I was being a character from a book.

TOM: 'Call me Count'?!

ELLEN: So?

TOM: So how many fucking counts do we know Ellen?

Beat.

ELLEN: Where are your bruises from?

TOM: I … he …

He hasn't, done something … to you?

ELLEN: Done what? For fuck's sake. Just fucking tell / me.

TOM: I can't!

I'm trying, I …

If I say it …

I think about him. Okay? Yes, I …

I know that sounds … I like him. I think. I can't explain it, I don't want to but I

I'm just trying to be … (honest)

I think about him. I can't stop … I see him every day and I …

He has this hold. Over me.

It's like … Like I want his approval or his attention or …

Something has happened. Not what you think but … I can't explain it, I can't make sense of it, but it's

I love you. You're the one I

But now it's like I can only

I can only feel good if I'm around him.

Beat.

I didn't ask for this.

ELLEN: So stop it. Make it stop.

TOM: I can't.

ELLEN: You could. You could quit your job. You could leave. We could leave here tonight. You don't have to see him anymore. You don't ever have to see him again.

>   *Beat.*

TOM: But I want to.

>   *Beat.*

ELLEN: Does he love you?

TOM: No. No, he doesn't. I know that. He couldn't. I think he … I think he hates me. This is what I'm trying to say. I think he hates all of us. It's like he has this … power. It's not … normal. He's … he's all hate. He's all cold and hollow and … it sucks you in but he's terrifying, he's, I think he's … Ellen. I don't think he's human.

>   *Beat. Maybe this is the moment where everything falls into place and* ORLOK *is revealed and no-one else has to die. Or maybe not.*

ELLEN: Of all the fuckwit bullshit / I've heard.

TOM: No, / please

ELLEN: You're absolutely fucking him.

TOM: No, I'm / not.

ELLEN: This is so / fucked up

TOM: You're not listening to me!

SCENE FIVE starts to encroach: Even later that night. KNOCK'*s office.* KNOCK *is bent double, sick, in pain. There is a spider, trapped under a glass.*

ELLEN: Just be honest!

TOM: I am!

>   *Beat.*

ELLEN: I don't believe you.

>   ELLEN *exits.* TOM *is thrust into:*

KNOCK: He's not here.

TOM: What are you doing?

KNOCK: I have to wait.

TOM: I thought it was a nightmare. I thought. But I have (marks). I have proof. Look.

KNOCK: Don't.

TOM: He's marked me.

KNOCK: Don't show me.

TOM: You have them too. I've seen it.

KNOCK: Don't come any closer.

TOM: I didn't know what I was seeing. He told me it wasn't real and I believed him. He told you it was a nightmare, same as me.

KNOCK: We're not the same.

TOM: He said it was nothing. That you / were nothing.

KNOCK: He said I'd have everything.

> *Beat.*

Yes. I believed him.

TOM: There are others, aren't there?

KNOCK: No.

TOM: I thought it was just me.

KNOCK: He promised / he wouldn't.

TOM: We let him in. But we can confront him.

KNOCK: I can't.

TOM: We can go to the police. We have proof. He'll never stop. Please. Knock. James.

KNOCK: I'm not allowed.

TOM: ?

KNOCK: I have to wait here. The spider. I have to wait. I have to wait for him, he said. I can't have it. Not till he gets here. I have to wait I have to wait for him I have to. But it's almost morning, so he might not, he might not. And the tiny feet tapping tapping tap tap tap tap tap. Can you hear it?

TOM: … No.

KNOCK: That's good. That's good.

> *He takes the spider out of the jar and dangles it by a leg.*

He'll be so angry.

SCENE SIX starts to encroach: The next night. ORLOK *and* KATE *in Kate's clinic.* KATE *is drinking.*

KNOCK: There are more flies, have you seen? Since the vines? More flies. More spiders. More birds. All the way up the chain. There's a llama. Have you seen? Just outside town. Someone bought a llama.

ORLOK: You're sitting in the dark.

KATE: It was light when I sat down.

ORLOK: It's late now.

KNOCK: I've been seeing just how much everything is alive.

> KNOCK *eats the spider.*

> *Through the following,* KNOCK *and* TOM *exit.*

KATE: Why are you here?

ORLOK: I heard about your mother. I wanted to give my sympathies.

> *Perhaps* ORLOK *moves to where the blood tests are kept, considers his options.*

KATE: How did you know where I was?

ORLOK: I thought work might be a good distraction.

KATE: I'm being hostile.

ORLOK: Not at all.

KATE: I don't have the energy to be polite.

ORLOK: Grief is like that. A truth-teller. Has its uses.

KATE: I was trying. To work. I've lost some blood samples. I was trying to find out how.

ORLOK: And did you?

KATE: I found whisky.

ORLOK: I can go.

KATE: Stay. Sit. Have you seen James?

ORLOK: At the vineyard.

KATE: He's avoiding me.

ORLOK: Death doesn't suit everyone.

KATE: I should be more prepared.

ORLOK: It's always a shock. Even when you know it's coming.

KATE: What do you know about it? Sorry, I shouldn't (assume) … you're just young.

ORLOK: It was a long time ago.

KATE: … Your parents?
    Were you with them?

ORLOK: Yes.

KATE: You're lucky. Not lucky, / but

ORLOK: No, it is a privilege, to be there at the end.

KATE: I was so frustrated with her. Staying here. Fighting this losing battle. After my dad died we'd argue about it, I'd say come to Melbourne, why sit in the ruins?

But she would never leave. She believed that the earth could … That it had this strength. It wasn't this hippy, tree-hugging, it was war. She'd say, if you desecrate something long enough, eventually it will fight back.

ORLOK: I couldn't agree more.

KATE: Such a waste.

ORLOK: She was right. Look at it now.

KATE: The vineyard? I don't know. The mine was always making promises. A bandaid over a gaping wound. If it sounds too good to be true … No offence but she wouldn't have trusted you.

ORLOK: And you?

KATE: Did you cry? I haven't cried.

ORLOK: I … don't remember.

KATE: It can't have been that long.

ORLOK: Six hundred years.

Feels like it.

KATE: There's something strange about you.

I'm a bit drunk.

ORLOK: Don't apologise.

KATE: I wasn't. Do you want a drink?

ORLOK: I do. But I won't.

KATE: My dad was an alcoholic. Is that what you are?

ORLOK: Do you know why it's traditional to plant roses next to vines?

KATE: It's a warning. If there's disease, the roses catch it first.

ORLOK: The canary in the coalmine. Exactly.

ORLOK *turns to leave.*

SCENE SEVEN starts to encroach: Later that night. ORLOK *and* TOM *in Tom and Ellen's house. There is garlic, a cross fashioned from two bits of wood, and a wooden stake on the table.*

KATE: There are no roses in your vineyard.

ORLOK: What's the point? You'd all ignore the warning anyway.

Through the following, KATE *exits.*

TOM: I was coming to find you.

ORLOK: I heard.

ORLOK *takes a step forward.* TOM *picks up the cross and garlic and holds them out.*

TOM: Stay back.

ORLOK *fakes a flinch, then laughs.*

ORLOK: You've been reading. Good for you.

TOM: I know what you are.

ORLOK: I can see that.

TOM: I know what you've done.

ORLOK: I saved the town, Tom. Just like you asked.

TOM: All those people, everyone who's missing.

ORLOK: Yes.

TOM: You're not denying it.

ORLOK: I've never lied. Not to you.

TOM: You tricked us.

ORLOK: I drank your blood. I don't know how I could have been more blatant.

TOM: You wiped my memory.

ORLOK: No. You did that.

TOM: [*re: the cross and garlic*] Why isn't this working?

ORLOK: Maybe you're not close enough.

ORLOK *begins to advance on* TOM.

TOM: Are you ... really here?

ORLOK: Ah. I've got in your head. That's interesting. Don't worry, it happens. I hope it wasn't anything too inappropriate.

TOM: I know everything.

ORLOK: Tom, with the soldier's heart.

TOM: I can expose you.

ORLOK: It was fun while it lasted, wasn't it? The surrender.

He plucks the garlic from TOM*'s outstretched hand.*

Garlic. Honestly.

TOM: But the cross. You you asked about there being no church here.

ORLOK: I have a genuine interest in town planning.

TOM: This isn't funny.

ORLOK: It's a question of belief. Do you believe in the cross as a symbol of God? Of holiness. Of purity. Of forgiveness. As a protection against all the evils of the world?

TOM: … No.

ORLOK: Do you believe in me as a manifestation of those evils?

TOM: I … don't know.

ORLOK: So here you are. Just a grown man holding a stick.

TOM: But the myths, the / stories.

ORLOK: You know what it's like, someone starts a rumour, a few thousand years later it's taken on a life of its own. The cross has a basis in fact: religion is my natural enemy, though people are rather secular these days if you stick to the right countries.

> ORLOK *takes the cross from* TOM *and tosses it aside. He picks up the stake.*

And this is meant to be a stake, is it? You'll need much more of a point than this. Doesn't have to be wood though, a knife will do, as long as it's straight through the heart. Allow me.

> ORLOK *takes a knife from the kitchen then holds* TOM *by the neck, the knife against* TOM's *throat.*

The cross thing annoys me, actually. Any religious symbol would do if you truly believed. Christians. The most frustratingly sure of their own superiority. Honestly Tom, I'm disappointed. Surely you didn't buy something so prosaically Western?

> TOM *is choking.* ORLOK *releases him.*

I'm sorry. I forgot it was you who wanted to kill me.

> *He hands* TOM *the knife.* TOM *doesn't do anything with it.*

Quickly then.

TOM: You changed Knock.

ORLOK: [*correcting*] Made him. The knife, Tom.

TOM: Why not me?

ORLOK: I told you. The first night we met. You're not enough.

TOM: I brought you here. I started this.

ORLOK: And there's still time to be a hero.

> ORLOK *uses* TOM*'s hands to press the point of the knife against his heart.*

TOM: It's my fault.

ORLOK: So redeem yourself.

> *Maybe* ORLOK *starts pushing the knife in himself.*

That's it. You're being very courageous.

TOM: My soldier's heart.

ORLOK: Yes, but that doesn't mean strength, it means a willing sacrifice.

> TOM *drops the knife.*

TOM: I can't.

SCENE EIGHT starts to encroach: The next night. A town hall meeting. KNOCK *reads from a prepared statement. Maybe* ELLEN *is there.*

ORLOK: I know. I know, it's okay. It's okay.

> *He cradles* TOM*'s face in his hands.*

KNOCK: The mayor's office is and always will be your only reliable source of information for ongoing police matters.

ORLOK: Look at you. No defences. The sheer terror in your eyes.

KNOCK: Do not believe sensationalised reporting.

ORLOK: I am sorry.

KNOCK: There are those who would seek to discredit this town. To drain us of hope.

ORLOK: I should have let you have your cross, your garlic. The illusion of safety is so important.

TOM: Why?

ORLOK: Panic really ruins the flavour.

> ORLOK *breaks* TOM*'s neck. Through the following,* ORLOK *exits.*

KNOCK: Let me reassure you that police are treating all reports seriously, but unrelatedly. This will be the last you hear from me on such baseless allegations.

> *Perhaps the cracks start to show here.*

As to the alleged disappearance of my

Tom, my colleague, and friend

Of course if I was concerned for his safety

If I thought that my actions could help him in any way, then I would

I would do everything in my power.

We are a small, but strong, community, and we will not be broken.

Blood is thicker than water. In fact, blood is life. And loyalty is

Loyalty is everything.

I will not be taking (questions)

He puts the statement down. As he starts to betray Orlok, the effect is physical.

I have only ever wanted the best for

I promised I'd do anything to save this town.

Please, for your own safety …

His professionalism returns.

For your own safety, I am issuing a curfew, effective immediately. Residents are not permitted to leave their house for any reason between sunset and sunrise.

SCENE NINE starts to encroach: Tom and Ellen's house. Just after the following dawn.

KNOCK: This is

I expect this will be the last you hear from me.

Maybe: he throws up blood.

KATE: How long?

ELLEN: Twenty-nine minutes.

KATE: You should—

ELLEN: I'll wait till thirty. That's what we're doing.

KATE: It's almost light.

ELLEN: Come away from the window.

KATE: I'm just looking.

ELLEN: Can you see anyone?

KATE: A couple (of people). Shall I call James again?

ELLEN: He won't answer. Sit down.

KATE: I think I know what it is.

ELLEN: You're making me nervous.

KATE: The vines. That smell.

ELLEN: Manure.

KATE: Something rotting.

ELLEN: Thirty.

ELLEN *dials a number on her phone. She waits. She hangs up.*

KATE: ?

ELLEN: Message bank full.

KATE: It's still ringing?

ELLEN: Straight to voicemail.

KATE: Call the police again.

ELLEN: They already know everything.

KATE: But you should tell them what he said.

ELLEN: There were things here. In the house, when I got back. There were

A cross. A cross and

He's dead, Kate? Okay? Tom's dead.

KATE: You shouldn't say that.

ELLEN: He tried to warn me, he tried to tell me something. I didn't listen and now it's too late.

KATE: If you believe that. If you really… what the fuck are we doing? Why are we just sitting here?

ELLEN: The sun's up.

SCENE TEN starts to encroach: That night. The tarn. KNOCK *has blood on his shirt.*

KATE: I'm going out there.

ELLEN: You can't.

KNOCK: You shouldn't be here.

KATE: [*to* KNOCK] Everyone needs to stop telling me what to do.

ELLEN: I haven't written your mum's obituary yet. I'll do it today.

KNOCK: It's not safe.

ELLEN: While there's still time.

Through the following, ELLEN *exits.*

KATE: I've been calling you.

KNOCK: I know.

I don't want to lie to you.

KATE: About what?

KNOCK:

KATE: Do you know something? About mum? Have they found her body?

KNOCK: No. No, they haven't.

KATE: Then what? Is it Tom? This curfew. You've got everyone panicked.

KNOCK: They should be.

KATE: Why?

KNOCK: You shouldn't be out on your own.

KATE: I'm not.

Beat.

What's that on your shirt?

KNOCK: There was a rabbit.

KATE: What?

KNOCK: A pest. Pests are okay, aren't they? Pests are acceptable. It starts small, that's the problem. That's how you convince yourself. Just a fly, a pest, a possum, a cat, a dog. But it only ends one way. A sheep, a pig, a cow, not enough. You need more, better, stronger. Human. That's the order. The inevitable. Anything else would be unnatural.

KATE: Is that blood?

KNOCK: It's not safe here.

KATE: Why is there blood on your shirt?

KNOCK: You're only safe in the daytime.

KATE: What is it that I should be afraid of?

Who is it?

KNOCK: Please. Just go home.

KATE: Why are you here? Did you know where I was? Did you follow me?

KNOCK:

KATE: It's not possible.

It's not because you're my friend. You're my ... So if you knew something. If you'd done something. To my mum. To Tom. I would know. You would have said something, you would have told me.

But Ellen has this theory. This wild theory. She thinks people aren't just missing, they didn't just leave. There's some sort of serial killer. Someone in authority, probably. And that's completely ridiculous. We would have known, we would have done something, if people were dying. But you have blood on your shirt and a look on your face like …

That's not possible because you've been there for me and you've comforted me and I spoke to you about my mum and my fears and you listened like you cared like you understood and we loved each other once, didn't we? So it wouldn't be possible for you to be someone else, someone completely different.

Or have I just been so wrapped up in my own grief and my own world and my career and my life and you. I've been thinking about you, so much, so pathetic. I haven't been paying a second of attention to what's going on around me. I've just been waiting and waiting for the worst thing to happen and then when it finally happened I was more upset that I hadn't heard from you. I hate myself. I'm not thinking, I'm not seeing the right things. How dare you, how dare you steal that from me. Steal my thoughts. And then disappear.

And now there's blood on your shirt and what the fuck have you done? What have you done to her? She was an old woman. A defenceless … She was … And Tom? And the others. How many others? And you're issuing curfews, what is that? It can't be true. It can't be. But there is blood. There is blood on you. You can't even look at me.

You tell me, right now. You tell me what you've done. You tell me whose blood that is. Stop avoiding stop ignoring stop talking in riddles and pathetic excuses, go fuck yourself, you fucking look me in the eye and you tell me everything you liar, you fucking coward.

Beat.

KNOCK: You're so … loud.

Something here. She hits him and he lets her. Or maybe he catches her arm and there's a brief moment before he lets her go.

Not your voice, but. Yes, your voice too. But your breathing, your pulses, the way your hairs scrape against each other, that screech like metal on metal. And your blood. Your endless blood. The way it rushes in your veins, it's the tide, pulling me in.

KATE: What are / you … ?

KNOCK: It's rabbit's blood. On my shirt. I told you.

I wanted to see you again. I knew that I shouldn't. Just one last time. But I shouldn't because I have this hunger. So I picked up the rabbit, I ripped it open and I drank its blood. But it's not enough. It will never be enough.

I didn't kill those people but I could have, I might as well have, I would like to. They're all loud, like you.

But Kate, I'm not loud anymore. I'm completely silent. And it's unbearable, because I can hear all of it. Smell all of it. It's rich, intoxicating. I can't see you because it's too much. The cracks in your fingers, the wet of your eyeballs, the salt of your sweat. I can taste your skin from here.

And I need your noise. I need to have it near me, inside me. I can't stop it. I don't want to stop it. I'm going to give into it.

SCENE ELEVEN starts to encroach: Later that night. ORLOK *in the vineyard, digging a grave.*

KATE: … James …

KNOCK: Run!

He lunges for her. She bolts. KNOCK *is thrust into:*

ORLOK: Finally. I've been waiting.

KNOCK: I needed time.

ORLOK: You could have had all the time in the world.

KNOCK: I'm sorry.

ORLOK *hands the spade to* KNOCK.

ORLOK: Dig.

KNOCK: If you'll let me / explain …

ORLOK: I said: dig.

KNOCK *starts digging.*

It was very simple. Total loyalty, that was all I asked.

KNOCK: It's too much.

ORLOK: Too much? For immortality?

KNOCK: I'm grateful, but this thing you've / done to me

ORLOK: This thing? This thing?!

KNOCK: It feels like punishment.

ORLOK: It's a gift! Power, eternity. You wanted to be like me.

KNOCK: But I'm not. I'm sick, I'm starving, all the time. I'm not in control.

ORLOK: You would have learned, I was teaching you.

KNOCK: I can't kill people.

ORLOK: Can't you?

You knew what I was offering and you welcomed me. You didn't care where prosperity came from, as long as it came.

KNOCK: You killed Tom.

ORLOK: Tell me, how does someone so mediocre inspire so much devotion?

I thought you were ready. I thought I could trust you.

KNOCK: You can.

ORLOK: Fucking dig!

KNOCK *digs faster.*

You're all so small. So fickle.

KNOCK: You could just let me go.

ORLOK: I despair of you.

KNOCK: Please. I won't tell anyone.

ORLOK: I know.

KNOCK: I'll be good. I promise.

ORLOK: To sire someone, create them and have them turn on you. Betray you. Your own son. Flesh tearing from bone. It hurts. And I haven't hurt in centuries.

KNOCK: I can do anything. I can dig. I can dig forever. Anything you want. What do you need? You need me to kill someone? I can try. I can do that. Kate. I can kill Kate, if you need me to, if that's what you want. I won't say a word. Cut out my tongue. I'll cut it out. Is that what you need? I won't go anywhere. Cut my legs off. Is that what you want?

ORLOK: You can stop digging.

KNOCK: No. Please.

ORLOK: It's ready now.

KNOCK: Just a little longer.

ORLOK: Come here.

SCENE TWELVE starts to encroach: Even later that night, towards dawn. ELLEN *in her house.*

KNOCK *stops digging. He goes to* ORLOK.

ORLOK *plunges his hand into* KNOCK*'s chest and rips out his heart.* ORLOK *pushes* KNOCK *into the grave and tosses the heart aside. Where it lands, the vines grow.*

ORLOK *casually walks to the table in Ellen's house and sits down, relaxed.* ELLEN *stays standing.*

ELLEN: Where is he?

ORLOK: How do you normally start?

ELLEN: Tom. Where is he? Please tell me.

ORLOK: Don't do that.

ELLEN: Where's his body?

ORLOK: You can't jump to the middle. What about the formalities?

ELLEN: I need to see him.

ORLOK: My name, age, occupation.

ELLEN: I have to know.

ORLOK: You're not even recording.

ELLEN: I need to know that he's really—

ORLOK: He's really.

Now sit, record. Get some background. Isn't this what you've been wanting? Interview with the vvventure capitalist.

ELLEN:

ORLOK: Come on. Play with me.

ELLEN: He's in the vineyard, isn't he? They all are. That's how the vines grew.

ORLOK: Why are you asking if you already know?

ELLEN: How did you make it do that?

ORLOK: The land had the taste for blood already.

ELLEN: What is that, some sort of revenge?

ORLOK: It's a talent, not a cause. You haven't asked about my childhood.

ELLEN: So what's the point?

ORLOK: You haven't even asked me where I'm Count of. I ran a country. Does that not interest you?

ELLEN: Counts don't run countries.

ORLOK: Voivode, actually. I'm translating. And yes, we do. Prince
    might be closer, ruler, warlord. But I thought Count had a certain
    elan, don't you agree?

ELLEN: … If you were going for entitled cosmopolitan elite.

ORLOK: No-one questions old money.

ELLEN: I did.

ORLOK: In the beginning. Never lasts, not with your lot.

ELLEN: Journalists?

ORLOK: Humans.

ELLEN: And you're not human.

ORLOK: No, I can fly and turn into fog. What are you bringing to the
    table?

ELLEN: I have to go to the vineyard.

ORLOK: Guilt and anxiety, how enthralling.

ELLEN: I have to find him.

> *She starts to leave.*

ORLOK: He's not with the others.

ELLEN: … Where is he?

ORLOK: Stay. And I'll tell you.

> *She hesitates, then sits. She starts her phone recording and puts
> it on the table.*

Excellent choice.

ELLEN: You're not giving me a choice.

ORLOK: There's a choice. Just not the one you think.

   Now, you have questions. Ask them.

ELLEN: How many? How many dead?

ORLOK: What did you say? Twenty? Thirty? That's conservative.
    At least twenty on the way here. No-one obeyed that curfew, did
    they? I left their bodies in the street this time. Thought I'd …
    change it up.

ELLEN: Is that true?

ORLOK: See for yourself.

ELLEN: Why us? Why here?

ORLOK: Small town Australia is dying, I like to help it along where
    I can.

ELLEN: Tom knew. And Knock.

ORLOK: In their own ways.

ELLEN: What did you do to Tom?

ORLOK: Are you jealous?

ELLEN: You manipulated him.

ORLOK: I drank from him. But I didn't trick him, not with any sort of 'magic' if that's what you mean. Knock I offered money and power. Honestly it's almost not worth being supernatural these days.

ELLEN: Did Tom want power too?

ORLOK: No, he was desperate for something else.

ELLEN: To be the hero. The town saviour.

ORLOK: I was going to say: love.

ELLEN: … He had love.

ORLOK: Not enough.

ELLEN: And what do you get?

ORLOK: I eat well.

ELLEN: That's it?

ORLOK: What more is there?

ELLEN: How do I know any of this is real?

ORLOK: You want me to kill one in front of you? You want to see the blood drain from its limbs?

ELLEN:

ORLOK: You're tempted.

> ORLOK *takes a wine glass. He bites his wrist and bleeds into the glass.*

ELLEN: What are you doing?

ORLOK: Why do you think you're here?

ELLEN: My interview.

ORLOK: Yes. I've been interviewing you for some time.

ELLEN: … For what?

ORLOK: In battle, you always leave one person alive. To tell what they've seen. The horror. The terror. The blood running in the streets.

ELLEN: What the fuck / are you …

ORLOK: I have to choose the person very carefully. I've been waiting so long for the right one. Someone with a voice. Someone unafraid to forge their own path, who won't bow to authority, who would endeavour to make the truth known no matter how … troublesome.

ELLEN: Someone to tell your story.

ORLOK: Stories are the only proof that we existed.

ELLEN: Your legacy.

ORLOK: History itself.

ELLEN: So that's me.

ORLOK: No that's Kate.

Beat.

ELLEN: Kate?

ORLOK: Jealousy. It'll be your undoing.

ELLEN: I'm recording, I have proof.

ORLOK: Yes. How's that going?

He picks up her phone, plays back a section of the recording. We can hear ELLEN, *but where* ORLOK*'s voice should be there's only silence.*

ELLEN: I could go to the police, I could tell them everything.

ORLOK: Good luck with that.

ELLEN: Why Kate?

ORLOK: She's a truth-teller

ELLEN: And I'm what? A liar?

ORLOK: You're chaos.

ELLEN: Fuck you.

ORLOK: It's not a criticism.

ELLEN: Are you going to kill me?

ORLOK: Yes.

But it's up to you what happens after.

Maybe he hands her the glass of blood.

Take, drink.

ELLEN: And be like you?

ORLOK: Humanity's beneath you.

ELLEN: I don't want to die.

ORLOK: You think you're living now? Down here, at the bottom of the chain.

ELLEN: Are you doing something to me?

ORLOK: That's your own desire you're feeling.

ELLEN: Tell me what it's like.

ORLOK: To feed?

ELLEN: To kill.

ORLOK: Euphoric. Untamed. A wave on the edge of breaking.

ELLEN: And after?

ORLOK: You're sated.

>   For a while.

ELLEN: Sounds animal.

ORLOK: Exactly.

ELLEN: Total freedom.

ORLOK: Forever.

ELLEN: With you?

ORLOK: Yes.

ELLEN: Partners.

ORLOK: I would teach you, train you, impart everything I know.

>   *Beat. Orlok's spell breaks a little.*

ELLEN: … So I'd be your student?

ORLOK: It's a great honour.

ELLEN: Sounds like an eternity of being patronised.

ORLOK: You're newborn. You'd need to be taught.

ELLEN: I don't need anything. Anyone.

ORLOK: You think you could do / this without me?

ELLEN: Why did Tom get to you so much?

ORLOK: … He didn't.

ELLEN: You didn't turn him. But you kept him alive.

ORLOK: He was my access to the town.

ELLEN: Only at first.

ORLOK: He had no memory. And he tasted incredible. But you know that.

ELLEN: You liked him.

ORLOK: Everyone liked him.

ELLEN: That bothered you. You buried him separately. His own grave.

ORLOK: A bargaining chip.

ELLEN: He was special.

ORLOK: No.

ELLEN: You wanted to learn from him. To be good. To be liked.

ORLOK: I can't think of anything more tragic than wanting to be liked.

ELLEN: Yet you risk exposure, death, to hang out in Bluewater and play vintner.

ORLOK: That's the game.

ELLEN: You were lonely. You fell in love with some average, small town boy and you followed him here like a lost puppy.

ORLOK: Your story, not mine.

ELLEN: You didn't have the guts to do what needed to be done.

ORLOK: I killed him. Broke his neck right where you're standing.

ELLEN: You could have destroyed this town in a day.

ORLOK: I like to take my time.

ELLEN: All this formality.

ORLOK: People let me do anything I want. They know they shouldn't, they know it's bad for them. But they ignore and deny and they let me in anyway. That's real power.

ELLEN: I pity you.

ORLOK: You could never do what I do. You could never be as good as me.

ELLEN: I could be better.

ORLOK: Prove it.

She drinks the blood.

He takes her in his arms. A moment, like they're about to kiss, then ORLOK *pulls back.*

ORLOK: He's under the house.

ELLEN: Who is?

ORLOK: You're perfect.

He bites her neck.

Dawn has broken.

KATE *enters, unnoticed by* ORLOK *and* ELLEN *who are completely engrossed in each other.*

KATE: Ellen!

What the fuck have you done?

KATE *runs to* ORLOK, *tries to pull him off* ELLEN. *He grabs her arm but keeps feeding. The life drains from* ELLEN, *she falls to the floor.* ORLOK *steps back.* KATE *grabs for the back door.* ORLOK *sees what she's about to do.*

ORLOK: No!

> KATE *flings the door open. Sunlight streams in, onto* ORLOK. *He bursts into flames. When the smoke clears, he's gone.*

> KATE *runs to* ELLEN.

KATE: Ellen. Ellen, wake up. Wake up.

> KATE *checks* ELLEN*'s pulse, she's dead.*

No. Fuck.

> *She gets out her phone, calls triple-0.*

Ambulance. It's my friend, she's … I heard shouting and I came out and she's, she's been attacked, she's … But there are, there are others. There are bodies in the street. Please hurry she's …

> ELLEN *wakes with a start.*

She's awake.

EPILOGUE

The land is desolate again.

Night. Ellen's house, things in disarray. ELLEN *is packing a bag. The book of demons is on the table.* KATE *stands in the doorway, holding a knife.*

KATE: Where are you going?

ELLEN: Kate. You scared me.

KATE:

ELLEN: I was packing. Didn't you hear the town's closing? Will you go back to Melbourne? I'm flying tonight.

KATE:

ELLEN: We should have known it was in the water.

KATE: You can't leave.

ELLEN: Probably been making us sick for a long time.

KATE: I can't let you leave.

ELLEN: Stopping us sleeping, don't you think?

KATE: I know what happened to you.

ELLEN: Clouding our judgement, making us see things that aren't really there.

　　Do you think it was the bodies that poisoned us? Or the mine or … ? Maybe after the vines died. Some sort of toxin, killing the land.

KATE: He killed the land, the town.

ELLEN: Useful isn't it? To blame him.

KATE: I should have told the police that night.

ELLEN: No-one would believe you.

KATE: It's the truth.

ELLEN: What's one more denial now?

KATE: Ellen. I don't want to hurt you. But I'm not going to let anyone else die.

　　ELLEN *leans forward to pick up the book,* KATE *flinches, holds the knife out. Maybe* ELLEN *laughs.*

ELLEN: Thought you might want this back.

ELLEN *holds the book out.* KATE *slowly takes it, holding the knife out.*

KATE: Is this a confession?

ELLEN: It's just a story.

KATE: You can hear it, can't you? My heart, my blood.

Beat.

ELLEN: Can smell your fear too.

KATE: You can't control it, the hunger.

ELLEN: I'm perfectly in control.

KATE: You must be starving.

ELLEN: Careful.

KATE: Here.

KATE *uses the knife to cut her hand. It bleeds.*

ELLEN: You're out of your mind.

KATE: I'm just showing you who you are.

ELLEN: And who the fuck are you? Put the knife down.

KATE: Straight through the heart, right?

ELLEN: I'm giving you a chance to walk away, Kate.

KATE: You're not squeamish are you?

ELLEN: Are you enjoying this?

KATE: It's just a little blood.

KATE *lets her blood drip onto the floor.* ELLEN *watches.*

ELLEN: Well don't waste it.

ELLEN *lunges for* KATE. KATE *thrusts the knife towards* ELLEN. *Just as they are about to collide:*

Blackout.

THE END

.

www.ingramcontent.com/pod-product-compliance
Lightning Source LLC
Chambersburg PA
CBHW050020090426
42734CB00021B/3348